DEAR FRIEND

DAILY 💙 NOTES
for Contemplation,
Connection, and Clarity

Michelle Maros
Founder of Peaceful Mind Peaceful Life®

Dear Friend

Copyright © 2025 Michelle Maros

All rights reserved. No portion of this book may be reproduced, stored in a retrieval system, or transmitted in any form or by any means—electronic, mechanical, photocopy, recording, scanning, or other—except for brief quotations in critical reviews or articles, without the prior written permission of the publisher.

Published by Harper Celebrate, an imprint of HarperCollins Focus LLC.

Author is represented by The Christopher Ferebee Agency, www.christopherferebee.com.

Any internet addresses (websites, blogs, etc.) in this book are offered as a resource. They are not intended in any way to be or imply an endorsement by HarperCollins Focus LLC, nor does HarperCollins Focus LLC vouch for the content of these sites for the life of this book.

Art direction and cover design by Sabryna Lugge

Interior design by Sabryna Lugge and Denise Froehlich

ISBN 978-1-4002-5262-6 (HC)
ISBN 978-1-4002-5263-3 (epub)
ISBN 978-1-4002-5264-0 (audio)

Printed in Malaysia

25 26 27 28 29 OFF 5 4 3 2 1

*For my mom, whose lifetime of love
notes has endlessly inspired me.*

―――――

*And for all my friends, near and far, who make
this world feel kinder and a little less lonely.*

CONTENTS

FOREWORD vii
INTRODUCTION xi

JANUARY 1
FEBRUARY 33
MARCH 63
APRIL 95
MAY 127
JUNE 159
JULY 191
AUGUST 223
SEPTEMBER 255
OCTOBER 287
NOVEMBER 319
DECEMBER 351

THANK YOU 383
ACKNOWLEDGMENTS 384
NOTES 385
ABOUT THE AUTHOR 386

FOREWORD

In 1984, I made the life-changing decision to check into a treatment center for bulimia. Over six weeks, I began a healing journey that still continues today. I learned to care for my body with mindful eating, yoga, and walking, while meditation and therapy helped me face my struggles. Little did I know, this was just the start of a transformation that would shape the rest of my life.

One year later, in 1985, my beautiful daughter, Michelle, was born. And in that moment, I felt a kind of hope that I had never known before—a hope for a life I couldn't have imagined, a life full of love, resilience, and possibility.

From the moment Michelle was born, I committed to parenting with emotional stability, drawing from my own struggles and therapy to develop a parenting style rooted in emotional support, affirmations, and the practice of mindfulness from the very start. I hung a handmade "feelings chart" on her bedroom wall and began each morning by asking, "How are you feeling today?" By the time she was three, we had a daily ritual: She would point to a feelings face, and we'd start the day grounded in understanding our emotions. I wrote inspirational messages on her bathroom mirror, reminding her daily of her worth and strength. And as she grew older, I shared words of wisdom from people who inspired me—messages of love, resilience, and courage—before she set out for school. These small, consistent practices became the foundation for a life of self-awareness and empowerment.

Over the past forty-one years, I've learned a powerful truth: How we begin our day shapes everything that follows. The intentions we set in the morning can create the energy that carries us through every moment. Starting the day with purpose is not just a practice—it's a deep commitment to ourselves, our growth, and living a life aligned with our highest potential.

As a mother, this has been my deepest aspiration: to equip Michelle with the tools and wisdom to build a strong, unshakable foundation within herself. I wanted to give her the strength to face life's challenges with grace and resilience, and the clarity to see herself and the world with love and courage.

We now understand that our mindset plays a pivotal role in how we respond to life's ups and downs. There's a Buddhist parable about two arrows: If we're struck by one arrow, it hurts. But we often add a second arrow, which is the suffering we create when we tell ourselves a story about why we got hit. If someone breaks your heart, that's the first arrow—it's painful. But the second arrow strikes when you start to believe you're unworthy or unlovable because of it. The truth is, you can be a kind, loving person and still experience pain. Life doesn't punish you for your heartache—it's simply part of the human experience.

I don't know you personally, but I believe you've picked up this book because, deep inside, you want to transform your life. You want to make your ordinary days extraordinary. You want to create a life that's infused with meaning and intention. So as you begin this journey of daily reminders and reflections, I invite you to pause and reflect on these three questions:

- What do I want to create today?
- What do I want to release today?
- What energy do I want to bring into the world today?

While we can't control every moment of every day, we do have the power to set the intention for how we show up in each moment. That's where our strength lies—our ability to decide how to respond, how to navigate life's challenges, and how to stay aligned with our true selves. This is how we cultivate our inner resilience and our power of choice.

In this beautiful book, Michelle continues the legacy of the practices we began together so many years ago. Through her words, she offers a steady stream of inspiration, wisdom, and love. May these messages guide you to begin each day with an open heart, a curious mind, and a deep belief in what's possible when you embrace your truest self. Let these words anchor you as you learn, grow, and step into your most authentic, unapologetic life. Michelle's gift to you is one of self-love, strength, and clarity—because, as she often says, "The relationship we have with ourselves is the foundation for everything we do in life. So make sure you love, accept, and trust yourself. And that begins the moment you wake up."

Michelle is the greatest blessing in my life. And now, as you turn the pages of this book, I know you're about to begin a transformative journey of loving-kindness toward yourself. With each passing day, you will step further into your most authentic self. Trust in this process. Let it unfold with patience and grace.

Every new day is an opportunity to begin again.

May you embrace it fully.

With blessings and love,

Barb Schmidt

INTRODUCTION

Since I was a little girl, I have had the vivid memory of sitting at the kitchen table with my mom before heading off to school. Life was always hectic growing up; like many families, we had places to be, and things often felt very rushed. Despite the chaos and busyness of the outside world, every morning before school, my mom would sit down to read me a daily inspirational passage. This set the tone for the day ahead and, if nothing else, gave me a sense of peace and hope.

My mom—more commonly known as "Peaceful Barb" these days—has been a meditator my entire life. She is a deeply spiritual person, so she shared these inspirational messages with me in hopes of making my daily lived experiences a little lighter and brighter, a little more grounded and centered.

These messages came from books, passages, and poems. Often, they felt perfectly aligned with my life, as if they were written specifically for me by someone who knew me well.

As time and my life unfolded, I've valued and treasured the practice of starting each day with inspiration. I have my mom to thank for that. Though we no longer sit at the kitchen table while I'm getting ready to head to school, we have created a platform and a nonprofit, Peaceful Mind Peaceful Life, to share daily insights, inspiration, and messages to help whoever may need a boost.

Life can be confusing and chaotic and uncertain, and we will never be able to control what happens in the world around us. Rather than letting this truth take me down, I like to remember that our power comes from being able to manage our reactions and responses to it all. This is the truth that gives me resolve, confidence, and conviction for each and every day.

My mom taught me early on that we can start to build inner resolve by establishing a strong foundation through practices like meditation and mindfulness. These practices have propelled me through difficult moments, trauma, and tragedy, and they have filled me with strength to weather so many of life's tumultuous storms. By starting each day in a connected, centered place, I set myself up for success, equipping myself with simple tools to tackle whatever comes my way.

By starting each day in a connected, centered place, I set myself up for success.

I've spent the past twelve years writing weekly inspirational blogs and sharing daily messages on social media. I never could have imagined that the seed planted within me at that kitchen table would bloom into a career of sharing, connection, and inspiration that would touch the lives of so many around the globe. Cultivating inspiration for this community is my life's work now, and I could not be more grateful and humbled to do it.

I've known for a long, long time that I wanted to translate my life's work into a book-length project. But I've had so many ideas and insights that I wanted to share, and it's been hard to put them all together in a way that makes sense to anyone else. When it came time to put pen to paper, I couldn't imagine my first book being anything other than an ode to my childhood and a passing of the torch of daily inspired living.

It's a realized dream to be able to share my thoughts, experiences, and insights on life with you, dear reader, every day, with the sincerest and deepest intention of shared connection, optimism, and, if nothing else, a bright spot on difficult days.

Though I'll never meet the countless people who've been touched by the work my mom and I have been doing, I've gotten to know this community of friends through the daily notes and letters we receive. I hope you feel like this book was written specifically for you—because it was—and that you feel connected to each passage, which has been handpicked with you in mind. As I pondered each entry, I thought of my younger self sitting at the kitchen table, soaking up those daily words to live by, and I wrote while sending this same feeling to you.

Use this book as a gentle guide for daily connection or even as a tool in your back pocket to rely on when life gets hard. It is my hope that whenever and wherever you open this book, you'll find exactly what you are looking for, and you'll feel the loving nudge from me, your friend, to remember that you are not alone. We can walk this journey of life together.

XO,

Michelle

JANUARY 1

NEW BEGINNINGS

Dear friend,

It has often helped me to think of life as a long, detailed novel, filled with many chapters. Each of our lives has a beginning, middle, and end, and everything in between provides twists, turns, and experiences that make our stories meaningful and unique.

With this perspective, you can start to reframe how you view the seasons of your life. Just like in your favorite book, chapters begin and chapters end; life is like this too. Anytime a chapter of life comes to a close, it's normal for feelings of anxiety and uncertainty to rise to the surface. It's natural to feel uneasy about the unknown. None of us can predict what will happen from moment to moment.

Even as you experience uncertainty, can you embrace the excitement of a new beginning? In life's transitions, be curious and invite wonder about what the next chapter will hold. Just like with your favorite adventure-packed novel, flipping the page to a new chapter can bring opportunity, surprise, and excitement.

Each new day—including today—is an opportunity to begin again, to choose differently, and to pursue new goals and ideals. How lucky are you to be writing this new entry of your life!

Remember, you have the power to start a new chapter and begin again.

KNOW YOUR VALUES

Dear friend,

When you hear the word *values*, what comes to mind? For most of us, values are introduced early in life—usually shaped by family, religion, or society. Growing up, I often felt like values were imposed on me rather than unearthed from me, which is why I rarely felt connected to them.

Tapping into what we value, from the inside out, offers our lives direction and deepens our purpose. Values are cornerstones of our lives, shaping our beliefs, transforming our thoughts, and influencing our words and actions. If we value kindness, everything we do will be infused with being kind. If we value honesty, the truth will always be at the forefront of our interactions.

If, somewhere along the way, you became disconnected from what you value, remember it's never too late to reconnect. To do so, ask yourself, *In this moment, what matters most to me?* From this simple question, you may find so many answers you seek. Try it today and see what you learn.

Remember, you are always changing, and so is your life. Let your interests and values transform with you.

GO AFTER IT

Dear friend,

Do you believe you deserve to have your dreams fulfilled? Do you actually let yourself pursue what you truly want? These might sound like silly questions because, instinctively, we probably answer with a resounding *yes*. Of course we go after what we want—or do we?

When I was a teenager, my dream car was a Jeep. But when it came time for me to buy a car, I never even went to look at one. To this day I feel sad when I see a Jeep on the road. In my reflection on these feelings, I unearthed a fascinating discovery: I've often allowed myself to have a deep desire but held myself back from making it a reality, dismissing my yearnings as unserious or impractical.

In the grand scheme of life, my car isn't that big of a deal, but it left me wondering: *What other desires am I subconsciously deferring? Do I not think I'm worthy of what I really want?* Asking myself these questions has been eye-opening. It's helped me clarify my wants, dreams, and goals and remind myself that I'm allowed to go after what I want, unapologetically.

Is there something you want deeply but don't allow yourself to have? Why not go after it today?

Remember, **you are worthy of your desires, and you're allowed to pursue what you want.**

YOU ARE NEVER A FINISHED PRODUCT

Dear friend,

The world encourages perfectionism. Whether we sense pressure from family, friends, or colleagues, it's normal to feel the push to be that "perfect" version of ourselves. Over time, our perfectionistic pursuits create a false sense of brokenness and write a story in our minds that we aren't enough and need fixing. We become burned-out and dejected, living in this vicious cycle of wanting to be *everything* to *everyone*—but somehow always falling short. Is it any wonder why? You were never meant to be *everything* to *anyone*. You are meant to be exactly who you are in the moment, imperfections and all.

Instead of dismissing this current version of yourself, can you seek to honor it? Start by embracing who you already are, knowing you are never a finished product. You are always becoming and evolving, never stagnant. Accept this powerful truth today, filling yourself with confidence and gratitude for who you are and excitement for who you will become.

Remember, **rather than trying to rush through this version of you, honor it, learn from it, and know that it's giving you what you need for the next chapter. You will evolve.**

JANUARY 5

FREE YOUR IMAGINATION

Dear friend,

Have you ever noticed how kids are endlessly creative? Their minds are filled with ideas, dreams, and wild imaginings. Do you ever miss living with that kind of openness?

Adulthood is consumed with checking things off our to-do lists and tending to endless responsibilities, and it often feels that the creative part is dormant or nonexistent. What if today is the day we wake it up?

Your mind is incredibly powerful and capable of creating so much if you allow it. Rather than judging your ideas as unreasonable or unrealistic or getting in your own way, allow your mind to run wild. Find inspiration and motivation through your imagination, moving forward in the path of your dreams.

Notice the joy that arises when your mind is allowed to imagine and create, unhindered by your own self-criticism. Embrace the fun that is available to you as you let your mind wander and wonder. Let yourself feel the thrill of the possibilities you envision.

Remember, **everything you create starts with a thought in your mind. Free your imagination from rules and limitations and uncover a whole new world.**

OUT OF YOUR HEAD

Dear friend,

Many years ago, I attended a yoga teacher training. During the hard parts of the class, our teacher would instruct us to "not think too much." He was encouraging us to go through the class grounded in our bodies, not in our minds. I've always been prone to overthinking, so this simple but powerful advice benefited me both on and off the yoga mat.

Despite wanting to at times, we can't turn off our minds, and we wouldn't really want to if we could. So what does "not thinking too much" mean, practically speaking?

For me, it means focus, presence, and connection with self. During uncertain times in my life, the conscious decision to step back, get out of my head, and connect with my heart has always brought me closer to the answers I was seeking.

You can live from the heart through daily connection with yourself, and you can start at any time. Today, try to find a few moments throughout the day to just be with yourself. Notice how it feels to be in your own company and listen for the whispers of your heart.

Remember, **your mind knows how to create, and your heart knows your truth. Let them both guide you through this day.**

JANUARY 7
YOU ARE NOT YOUR PAST

Dear friend,

    I think it's safe to assume that each of us has pieces of our past we wish we could erase. We know we aren't perfect people, but it's uncomfortable to remember the mistakes we've made, the harm we've caused, and the errors in judgment that have left us feeling shaken. These moments become painfully seared into our memories.

    If you've been holding on to memorable moments like these for too long, today I hope you can set yourself free from carrying these burdens of your past. Not a single part of your life defines who you are. You contain multitudes. You are energy, expression, action, and intention. Like the waves of the ocean, you rise, you fall, and you persist.

    If something is plaguing you from long ago, remember that none of us is born with all the answers. We learn through living and making mistakes. This is how we grow. So ask yourself, *What can I learn from my mistake? How can this error help me grow?* Let your answer be what you carry forward.

Remember, your past does not define you; only you have the power to name who you are.

DON'T REGRET YOUR LOVE

Dear friend,

Do you remember your first crush? Can you call to mind the excitement you felt when you had butterflies in your stomach? When you couldn't stop smiling? When a whole new world of joy opened in front of you?

Love and relationships are some of life's biggest blessings. What's more beautiful than feeling a strong connection with someone else, sharing memories and moments and intertwining your paths for a lifetime?

Still, not all relationships will stand the test of time; some are here for a reason but only for a season. No matter how long it lasts, try not to hold regret for the love you share with someone, because in that moment, it is exactly what you want and exactly where you are supposed to be.

Today, celebrate the love you've shared in your past, and find joy in the love you feel at present. No relationship, no connection, no love is ever wasted.

Remember, **you're allowed to evolve and grow out of relationships. The love you shared has purpose, and you're allowed to move on.**

JANUARY 9

LOOK FOR TINY JOYS

Dear friend,

    Do you consider yourself a joyful person? I know when asking myself this question, for much of life, I sadly answered with an exasperated *no*. I used to believe true happiness was out of reach, reserved for when I could tick those externally motivated boxes that I thought needed to be checked.

    If you find yourself putting off your joy and waiting to achieve some major benchmark in order to be happy, let me remind you: You always deserve to feel joy, and it is fully available to you right now.

    We don't need grand gestures and massive accomplishments to feel happy, fulfilled, and complete. Small moments every day can bring smiles to our faces and remind us that good can be found in each one.

    Joy is exponential; one joyous moment leads to another. When I seek the small joys in my everyday life, I set myself up for more success and fulfillment. My tiny joys live in my morning coffee; couch cuddles with my cat, Charlotte; and rewatching my favorite sitcom.

    You, too, can find comfort in the seemingly effortless moments of your routine and lean on those simple joys when times get tough.

Remember, **life is filled with little joys just waiting to be noticed. Those joys are your life rafts, lifting you out of hardship when you need it most.**

STAY OPEN TO POSSIBILITIES

Dear friend,

We try to control so much in life without realizing that almost nothing is in our control. I say this not to make you feel powerless but to remind you where your power actually lies: within you.

Of course, we want to be active participants in our lives: show up, make plans, and visualize our idealized outcomes. But how do we react when things don't go our way? Are we willing to accept and adjust? Or do we resist and fight back?

It's often human nature to white-knuckle through hard and unexpected situations, attempting to force our original plans into our ever-changing realities. But the truth is, most of the time, this resistance only prolongs the inevitable and causes unnecessary pain. Imagine the peace you could experience if you learned to release the need to control, especially when things don't go how you wanted them to.

When you try to micromanage every aspect of your life, you actually close yourself off from possibilities outside of your periphery. So if you're trying to tightly hold on to control, release the reins a little, and lean in to trust. Life can support you and surprise you when you least expect it; you just have to remain open to it.

Remember, **freedom is found in releasing control. Find ease and peace in letting life guide you.**

INFLUENCE AND INSPIRATION

Dear friend,

One of my greatest teachers, my mom, has always reinforced the idea that we are the company we keep. When we look within and do the deep work of self-reflection, building a strong connection with ourselves, we can know who we truly are. But as ever-changing human beings, it's only natural that we will be shaped by outside forces too. So who gets a say in your life?

Who you surround yourself with, where you take in knowledge, and the energy you cultivate in your life matter. Today, take stock of your environment and who influences you the most. Whether it's close friends, family, community, or the people you interact with virtually, notice who you engage with and how they make you feel.

We may not always have a say in who's in our sphere, and there will always be people around who don't align with our values and ideals, but remember to keep close the ones who do. It's up to you to build community and be inspired by those who light you up from the inside out.

Remember, **your energy is a precious resource; you get to choose who has access to and influence on it.**

TALK BACK TO STRESS

Dear friend,

Here's a known but frustrating truth: Life is stressful. It can often feel like we spend much of our waking hours thinking about stress: *How can I have less of it? How can I avoid it? And when it inevitably comes, how can I manage it?*

Lately, I've started talking back to my stress, and it's helped me immensely. When I'm having a particularly overwhelming day, I'll simply remind myself that I am capable of handling it. It sometimes sounds like, "Yes, this is hard and stressful, but I've got this." Or, the little reminder that no single stressful moment or thought will live with me forever often propels me forward. In short, rather than fighting the stressful nature of human existence, I've started to accept it.

Today, imagine how you can talk back to your mind when it spirals through the stresses of your life. Notice how it feels to push back against the narrative telling you that you aren't capable of managing the difficult moments of your day.

Remember, **you are strong, confident, and capable. You have everything you need inside you to manage life and the stresses that come with it.**

BECOME YOUR OWN BEST FRIEND

Dear friend,

I can imagine how much you value the relationships in your life—your friends, family, colleagues, and community. And you intend to show up for people and give love freely, and I know you make your people feel seen, heard, and understood. You are a good friend—loving and kind and supportive. So today, I ask: Are you a good friend to yourself too?

Do you extend the same compassion, empathy, and care to yourself as you give to the people in your life? Do you forgive yourself? Do you show yourself grace and unconditional love for who you are and who you're becoming? Most of us focus on being the friend everyone wants to have, while forgetting the supportive friendship we deserve to have with ourselves.

Becoming your own best friend means loving yourself when you feel unlovable, accepting who you are in the good times and bad, and being there for yourself in all the ways you would for anyone else. Ask yourself, *How do I want to be treated?* Listen for answers.

Remember, **you deserve your own friendship, kindness, care, and compassion. You are worthy of the kind of love you share with others.**

BE PROUD OF YOURSELF

Dear friend,

As kids, we sought ways to make the adults around us proud. Achieving that kind of pride felt special to me, like a cherry on top of a job well done. As adults, we don't always have the same opportunities to achieve this level of satisfaction, and I've found myself missing the feelings that come with it.

I often wonder why we reserve pride for the big occasions, celebrations, and milestones. Are our daily actions and deeds not worthy of pride too? Knowing how challenging life can be, don't we deserve to be proud of ourselves simply for showing up every single day?

The truth is, you don't have to wait to achieve pride or have it affirmed by someone else. You have the power to usher pride back into your life today!

Take note of your hard work and commitment. Call to mind the effort and energy you put into your life, your dreams, and your relationships. Remember how you bring care, kindness, and empathy to people. It matters how you show up in the world, who you are, and how you make others feel. Your life is always worthy of praise.

Remember, **you don't have to wait to feel pride; you are worthy of it right now.**

FROM NICE TO KIND

Dear friend,

For as long as I can remember, I desired to be *nice*. Being nice always seemed like the highest ideal anyone could embody, and as far as I could tell, it would guarantee widespread love and acceptance.

Imagine my surprise when I realized that being nice actually isn't the appealing trait I once admired. Niceness paves the way for people-pleasing and codependent behavior. It provokes inauthentic connection with hidden, often manipulative, motives. Being nice, I discovered, just didn't feel authentic.

I've since learned a simple but powerful distinction: I no longer want to be nice; rather, I seek to be *kind*. Where niceness grows from uncertainty and acts out of fear, kindness stems from the heart and leads with compassion. Kindness releases expectation, allowing life to unfold. Kindness rejects manipulation and replaces it with trust. Kindness is inclusive rather than exclusive.

Being kind isn't about being polite in order to be accepted. It's about showing and sharing real concern, and in living this way, you will receive actual love and acceptance. How can you transition from nice to kind today?

Remember, **your kindness is a virtue, and the world needs more of it.**

REMEMBER YOUR HUMANITY

Dear friend,

Do you ever find yourself craving the simplicity of the good ol' days? The romanticized version of life before everything seemingly became so challenging?

Division, disasters, global struggles . . . I often see memes begging for "precedented" times since we seem to be experiencing so many unprecedented ones! Recently, when I was stuck in this nostalgic loop, my mom responded back to me: "Life has always been difficult. None of this is new, but how we are responding to it is."

With these wise words in mind, how can we respond to the times we live in with compassion, understanding, and a connection to our shared humanity?

Rather than seeking what's going wrong, look for the similarities you share with those around you and make an effort to live in love.

When you live in love, you recognize the humanity in yourself and others. When you live in love, you are not judgmental, condescending, or hateful. When you live in love, you want what's best for all.

Even though we are all different, we are connected and share so much. Focusing on our similarities leads to empathy, kindness, understanding, and, ultimately, love.

Remember, **we are in this life together.**
Love will bridge our differences.

UNBLOCK YOUR SUCCESS

Dear friend,

I've come to the conclusion that self-doubt has been one of the biggest hindrances in my life. Patterns of insecurity and unworthiness have held me back and kept me stuck. They've been truly debilitating.

It took me a long time to realize the only person blocking me from the life I desired was myself. I had to decide that doubt would no longer play a role in my life, and I've worked relentlessly to untangle the hold it had in my mind.

Ask yourself today, *Am I holding on to any persistent doubts about myself and my abilities? Am I uncertain of my strengths? Do I over-emphasize my mistakes and underestimate my wins?*

Be gentle and forgive yourself for the doubts you've believed; we are so rarely taught how to be fully confident in ourselves and to love who we are. Give yourself the space to explore a life free from the anchor of self-doubt. Try to catch yourself in the act of holding yourself back or convincing yourself that you're not enough—and go for it anyway. The world benefits from your unique magic and wisdom.

Remember, you have purpose in this world. Don't let your mind tell you you're unworthy or not good enough.

DARE TO DREAM AGAIN

Dear friend,

Today, I encourage you to remember the yearnings of your childhood. Recall those feelings of excitement and imagination. Remember who you were before responsibility and expectation crowded out your dreams and got in your way.

When you think about your journey, about everything you've experienced up until this moment and everything you envision for the future ahead, how do you feel? What comes up for you when you let yourself pause and reflect on your path so far? How do you envision your path going forward? Contemplating these questions helps you remember the life you want, while also uncovering untapped, hidden desires and dreams.

Life is filled with distractions and detours; it's easy to lose sight of our paths. Today is the day to remember your purpose, power, and meaning in this world and to recommit to living on your own terms. Dare to dig up the dream life buried in your past. Don't let this harsh world make you believe you are worthy of less.

Remember, **your unique dreams are valid; you are allowed to pursue what lights you up.**

JANUARY 19

FIND SAFETY WITHIN YOURSELF

Dear friend,

When was the last time you felt truly safe? Was it with someone you love? In a place that felt like home? In an environment where you were treasured and appreciated?

I know a sense of safety can feel rare and precious; the world out there can often be scary. The uncertainty, the heartache, the loss, the sadness—they all lead us to believe it's unrealistic to feel true safety on a regular basis.

We can't rely on constantly changing external situations to bring us a sense of security. Instead, we must cultivate a strong, solid foundation that can fortify us from the inside out. When you build that safe place within yourself, you can visit it anytime you want.

So honor yourself today by becoming your own safe space. Seek to know yourself, love yourself, and trust yourself, and build an unwavering belief that you can handle anything life puts in your way. You know the world outside can never shake your foundation within.

Remember, **your true strength and security lie in how you relate to and honor yourself in every moment. You are stronger than you believe.**

CHECK YOUR PRIORITIES

Dear friend,

Do you know what matters to you? Do you know what you value and what you wish to achieve? If not, how will you know how to prioritize your time and energy, your most precious, valuable resources?

Today, you have so many choices to make. From the moment you wake up to the time you go to bed, you will encounter countless opportunities to choose and prioritize. Check in with yourself today and familiarize yourself with your guiding principles. In doing so, you'll find clarity on what you truly value.

As you move through the day, prioritizing yourself and your highest ideals, make choices from this space of clarity. This might mean pausing before you make your next choice—whether it's what you will eat for breakfast this morning or what you will listen to on your way to work.

Life is always changing, and nothing stays the same; this goes for you too. Be sure to keep tabs on yourself as you move through life, making adjustments and shifting when called to.

Remember, **your life and your choices matter. Give yourself and your place in this world the attention they deserve.**

JANUARY 21

YOU NAME WHO YOU ARE

Dear friend,

What do they think about me? If you've ever been curious about this, welcome to the club! It's easy to fall into these mental rabbit holes, wondering how others perceive and judge us. Similar to the way we form opinions about characters on television and in movies, we wonder how often people are judging us as we go about our lives.

None of us views life through the same lens. While sometimes frustrating and infuriating, it has brought me an odd sense of relief knowing that two people can stand in the same spot at the same time and have deeply different experiences. This has helped me release the need to uncover other people's perceptions and judgments about who I am, because I know that sometimes I can be misunderstood. No matter what, other people's opinions and judgments do not have the power to say who I am. And the same is true for you.

Today, take heart in knowing that other people's opinions of you will never be able to diminish your identity, purpose, and worth. You always have the authority to name who you are.

Remember, **who you are and how you show up in the world are entirely up to you. No one has the power to minimize your impact.**

TAKE INVENTORY OF YOUR LIFE

JANUARY 22

Dear friend,

During college, I worked a summer job at an airplane maintenance facility. I was the "parts girl," responsible for keeping an inventory of all the parts that went into airplane maintenance. This experience showed me how important it is to keep track of essential elements so that you're prepared for whatever comes your way.

Why do I share this? The same inventory concept applies to our personal lives too. When we take time to notice what we have, what we want, and what we need to do to get there, we can feel more confident in our choices.

Today, sit with yourself and review: Choose a year, season, or decade. Remind yourself of the successes and accomplishments, the tough lessons and hardships, and the desires and intentions you had during that time. Then ask yourself, *How has everything I have been through prepared me for where I am now? What goals and challenges lie ahead? What do I have and what will I need?*

This personal review will help you create a clear inventory of the parts that make you *you*—and this self-knowledge will take you far and allow you to be prepared for whatever comes next.

Remember, **the more you know, honor, and understand yourself, the more powerful and confident you become.**

JANUARY 23

HEALING THROUGH HUMOR

Dear friend,

When we think of healing, we probably imagine one of the following: medicine, doctors, or the deep emotional reflection and consistent work needed for internal relief. We can easily become overwhelmed by the immensity of it all.

While there are many paths to healing, a special kind of relief stems from happiness, laughter, and joy. What they say is true: Often, laughter is the best medicine.

You will experience incredible therapeutic benefits when you allow yourself to smile and find lightheartedness, despite the drama and trauma in life. This can come in the form of something you watch, something you listen to, or someone you're with.

In some of my darkest moments, levity from humor often lifted me up and propelled me forward. Is there anything better than the gift of unexpected laughter to help remind us of the dualities of life? If life is presenting you with unrelenting difficulty, ask yourself, *Where can I find an opportunity to laugh today?*

Remember, **laughter is medicine, and humor lifts spirits and can lead to healing.**

LIVE AN ALIGNED LIFE

JANUARY 24

Dear friend,

How we define the gold standard of living will look different for each of us. What I perceive to be my peak level of happiness and success will probably look completely different for you. Realizing this has been key in finding my own happiness.

I used to think that if I could live up to other people's expectations and benchmarks, happiness would somehow make its way to me. I was living from the outside in rather than the other way around. While I honor and respect the wisdom and guidance from those around me, the truth is, no one knows what it's like to live my life, and I don't know what it's like to live theirs. No one knows your heart like you do, and no one better understands your deepest desires.

Today, seek to live life on your own terms. Living a life that's true to you—aligned with who you are and what you want—will always lead you to where you want to be.

Remember, **by tuning in to what you want, every day, and making choices that coincide with your desires, you will never go astray.**

JANUARY 25

REWRITE YOUR INSECURITIES

Dear friend,

We all have aspects of our lives that make us feel embarrassed or insecure. One of mine has always been my extra-sweaty palms (or hyperhidrosis, to be technical). Since childhood, I've tried to hide my insecurity about this. In groups, I'd often cross my arms to hide my hands, anxiously wiping away any excess sweat. I often held myself back because I was afraid of ridicule or judgment. I've since learned that others perceived this behavior as standoffish or even angry—all because of my sweaty-palm insecurity!

What negative stories are you telling yourself about yourself? What's holding you back from being present and at ease in your daily life?

I hope my story can remind you that you have the power to release the insecurities you hold deep inside. You can change the script of the story you tell yourself about whatever you think is "wrong" or "different" about you. I hope you allow these aspects of yourself to teach you something instead. Be open to the possibilities and opportunities that arise from your curiosity. That is the real gift.

Remember, **you hold the power to rewrite any script that plays in your mind. If an insecurity is weighing you down, let today be the day you let it go.**

HONOR YOUR BOUNDARIES

Dear friend,

You've probably heard a lot about the importance of setting healthy boundaries. Even though it's a common practice, it's not always easy to set and enforce them in our lives. We know the benefits, but the anxiety of rocking the boat, alienating people, and rubbing someone the wrong way is very real.

Today, remember the power of setting boundaries, and consider reframing the role they play in your life. Boundaries are the ultimate signal of self-care, self-worth, and self-love. When you set a boundary, you are advocating for yourself and your needs.

This is not to say that making a significant life change will be easy. Changing a long-standing pattern, especially in relationships, is hard work. Human beings are complex, after all. But just think about how powerful and important this practice is!

If something isn't working in your life, you owe it to yourself and your relationships to speak about it and find a solution. Boundaries aren't a punishment. Caring for yourself doesn't mean you don't care for other people. You can set boundaries for yourself and still love and honor the people in your life.

Remember, **boundary setting is one of the most powerful acts of self-care. You never need to apologize for loving yourself.**

SEE THE GOOD IN CHANGE

Dear friend,

If you're a creature of habit like me, you likely find comfort in routines, and you're fond of the familiar. I find a sense of security in the things that stay the same, and for much of my life, I've resisted change. But as we know, the only constant in life *is* change.

If you want to create peace that lasts, it's important that you learn to become friends with change and be open to what it can teach you. Take some time to reflect on your past and recall a change you weren't exactly thrilled about. Did you resist it, or did you go with it? Are you stronger today because of it? How has your character shifted as a result?

Let this exercise in reflection remind you that you don't need to fear the unexpected twists and turns of life. Hold in your mind the moments when you handled change with strength and grace, and allow these memories to fuel your confidence for how you'll manage it in the future. You can approach every change with assurance and even optimism, reminding yourself that you have been through difficult circumstances before. With every bend in the road, you can rest easy, trusting that life's detours will propel you farther on your path.

Remember, **change is constant and always an opportunity for growth; embrace it.**

YOU ARE INFINITELY CREATIVE

Dear friend,

I've been known to doubt my creative attributes. I've downplayed my skills and perceived myself as average or unnoteworthy. High standards, expectations, and competition led me to make all-or-nothing judgments about myself. If I wasn't innately good at something, I closed myself off from it.

Can you relate?

Creativity is a quality we all possess. It adds color, emotion, and character to our lives. But as adults, it's not always easy to let ourselves play, create, and imagine without expectation. Creative acts can feel unproductive or even silly. But when we joyfully commit to being creative, we often uncover parts of ourselves that we didn't know were hidden within.

Today, affirm your unshakable, innate creativity. Imagine, dream, and explore. Let your mind wander. Each time you do, you fuel your creative fire. Be curious and receptive to people, places, and things that spark your creative flame, even if you don't know why. And most importantly, let your thoughts reinforce the magic that lives inside you. You have something unique to give to this world, and it lives within your ability to create.

Remember, **creativity is within you. You always have the power to tap in to it and unleash it.**

A POWERFUL LIFE LESSON

Dear friend,

I want to share with you a simple but powerful lesson my mom taught me years ago. This has been a game changer and a lifesaver in so many moments when things could have turned sour. It's an awareness tool that she learned during treatment for an eating disorder, and we still use it today.

What is this powerful tool? We use the acronym HALT as a reminder to check in with ourselves: *Am I hungry? angry? lonely? tired?*

My mom encourages me to pause whenever I find myself in an extremely reactive state. When I feel anxious, moody, or irritable—when I find myself prone to saying or doing things that I don't mean or that aren't helpful—I remember to HALT and check in. Because usually at least one of those four things is compounding the stress of my daily challenges.

The practice of HALT creates space to uncover what you need, from moment to moment. Sometimes all you need is to check in and care for yourself. Try checking in with HALT today when you're feeling out of sorts and see if it takes the pressure off.

Remember, **take time to check in and ask yourself what you need. You are always worthy of self-care and kindness.**

WHAT IS TRUE ACCEPTANCE?

Dear friend,

Is there a part of your life that you struggle to accept? Maybe you feel shame around your body, maybe you are at war with your career path, maybe you struggle to find the relationships your heart desires, or maybe you're frustratingly behind on a benchmark you've set for yourself.

It can be challenging to be human, staring down our lives that simply aren't how we'd like them to be. Frustrated, overwhelmed, and let down, we blame ourselves for our perceived inadequacies. Hopeless, we believe it will never change.

Consider how you would feel if you could simply accept everything in this moment—the good, the bad, all of it.

When you allow yourself to embrace your reality, rather than resisting it, you start to cultivate the strength, confidence, and awareness you need to make the changes your soul is asking of you. Staying present to who you are, you release the judgments and criticisms that have held you back or held you down. Radical self-acceptance requires practice, but it will provide peace of mind and clarity and initiate the forward motion you so desire.

Accept this truth today: You are already enough.

Remember, **through acceptance you become aware of the changes you wish to make.**

DON'T GIVE UP

Dear friend,

When everything feels like it's just too much, how do you find the motivation to persevere? How do you get through periods of overwhelming emotion and inner turmoil?

Perhaps you've started to tell yourself that you don't have it in you to go through any more, or maybe you're tempted to stop trying altogether.

If you're feeling this way today, or if you've ever felt this way, I hope you know you're not alone. Nothing is wrong with you. You are not the unlucky one in this world who has been left behind and forgotten. Your efforts and desires are valid and meaningful.

Just because life might be testing you in this moment, it doesn't mean there isn't a blessing around the corner. Keep your head up and eyes open to see it. Through challenges and struggles, you can learn to persevere during the painful times and remember that everything passes, eventually. Hang in there; good moments in abundance are on their way to you.

Remember, **no feeling is final. Everything is always changing. Don't ever give up.**

FEBRUARY 1

UNFINISHED BUSINESS

Dear friend,

Has a chapter of your life come to an end when you weren't ready for it to? When this happens to me, I'm often left yearning for closure. Something about unfinished business leaves us feeling rattled and unsettled. So let's take care of business today and close the loops on the parts of our lives that feel left open. There is no better time than the present, after all.

We aren't always given an opportunity to say and do the things we'd like. Life can be messy and complicated. But to some extent, you can take your life into your hands and complete the parts that still feel open-ended.

Ask yourself, *What situations in my life are plaguing me with anxiety and uncertainty?* I'm often faced with these gnawings late at night, when trying to sleep. The *why*s and *what if*s are a great place to dive in. Is there an action you'd like to take? Something you want to say? Know that you can find closure for yourself on your own terms.

Remember, **it's never too late to take the action you've been yearning to and start a new chapter.**

OUT OF A RUT

Dear friend,

Do you ever feel like you're living out the plot of the movie *Groundhog Day*? You wake up each day with the hope of something new, only to be faced with the same thing over and over. I've felt this way often. I've cursed the days when I felt stuck—as if no matter what I did, nothing would change.

There is richness in our routines; our self-care habits keep us on track with our larger goals as well as provide a sense of steadiness and calm. But what do we do when a routine becomes monotonous and mindless and unfulfilling?

Feeling stuck is a natural, normal part of life. And though spinning your wheels in a rut feels painful and frustrating, it can actually be rewarding. When you are present and attentive to them, ruts can offer useful information about what is no longer working in your life, which can help you to make the changes you crave and move you in the direction of your dreams.

If you're currently mired in a rut, don't fret! Embrace it as an opportunity for growth and change.

Remember, **feelings of stagnation can guide you toward the meaningful, transformational changes that your soul is begging you to make.**

WHO ARE YOU LIVING FOR?

Dear friend,

We often feed on external validation and praise. While receiving approval from others can provide momentary comfort, if we're too reliant on it, we can fall into people-pleasing and internal neglect. Of course, it's nice to feel noticed and appreciated, but what happens when we lose ourselves along the way?

Today, pay attention to your motives and intent. Are you taking action for yourself? Or for the appeasement of someone else? Is a person in your life holding court in your mind, subconsciously dictating the moves you make? Consider what it would take to live for you rather than for others.

Know that centering your needs isn't selfish but is a deep signal of respect for your unique life. Doing so raises the level of your own voice so that it doesn't get lost in the noise of others'. Can you seek to make choices inspired by your values, interests, and ideals? This is how you live on your terms.

Remember, **your life is yours, and it doesn't have to make sense to anyone else. Embrace your power of choice.**

UNDERSTAND TRUE FORGIVENESS

Dear friend,

I find that the practice of forgiveness is often misunderstood. Many of us are pressured to forgive before we're ready. We might hear, "Get over it, move on, it's not that big of a deal." Rushing the process encourages us to bypass our pain and emotions, disconnecting us from the situation.

Taking time to feel and reflect, though not always easy, paves the path for true freedom and forgiveness. So let's talk about what forgiveness really is. It's not casual acceptance or condoning bad behavior. It's the act of recognizing pain, feeling it, and following through with healing. Forgiveness is about releasing yourself from the past so you can be fully present to your life now.

Have you been holding on to something you're ready to let go of? Give yourself permission to witness your pain and acknowledge what has passed, with the intention of moving forward with healing. If, in the process, you find that you're not quite as ready as you thought you were, that's okay. Be gentle with yourself and start small.

Remember, **forgiveness is the act of acceptance, healing, and letting go.**

NOT REJECTION, BUT REDIRECTION

Dear friend,

It's not easy to hear the word *no*. This small word carries a painful punch and often sends us into spirals of self-doubt. Conceptually, we understand that we're destined to be turned away from opportunities and experiences; it's just the odds of life. Yet when it happens, it can feel crushing and defeating.

To help cope with the pain of rejection, consider this reframe: A no can be for your own good. I know that's probably difficult to read, because it was hard to write—even though I know it to be true! Rejection directs you away from what's not serving you. It both protects you from something that's not meant for you and guides you in a new, exciting direction. A closed door helps prepare you for a better one on the horizon. The roadblocks you face could simply be detours, leading you down wild and wonderful roads you never would have taken, to places you never would have seen.

A no to something good can lead to a yes to something great. How exciting is that?

Remember, it's not rejection; it's redirection. Trust that you are being guided toward something better than you can imagine.

THE VIRTUE OF VULNERABILITY

Dear friend,

A few years ago, I had an intuitive nudge to share more personal aspects of my relationship with grief. I allowed myself to write freely from my feelings and didn't second-guess how those feelings would be perceived. I hit Publish on my words before I could give myself a chance to back out.

Ripping off this Band-Aid and risking vulnerability opened my eyes to how powerful it can be. I was flooded with support and affirmation of my experience. I learned that my avoidance of vulnerability stemmed from fear: fear of judgment, fear of perceived weakness, fear of people knowing too much about me, fear of rejection.

While these fears are valid, they keep us from the beautiful experiences a vulnerable life can bring. Vulnerability creates opportunities for human connection. It breaks down barriers and walls. It evokes empathy and encourages more vulnerability.

Today, you might come upon an opportunity to wisely practice vulnerability and break down walls between you and another human being. Embrace your strength and lean in to the potential of life-changing connection.

Remember, **your vulnerability is powerful and a bridge to beautiful moments.**

THE IMPORTANCE OF SELF-REFLECTION

Dear friend,

In life's big moments—milestones, new beginnings, and endings—it's important to check in with yourself and be present to what life is bringing you. Self-reflection and introspection are powerful practices to keep you connected and present, helping you nurture the most important relationship in your life: the one you have with yourself.

As you come to meet yourself today, let go of the need to experience an epiphany or an aha moment. Simply commit to being you, carving out time to recharge your mind and soul. In self-reflection you can clarify what you seek and gain reassurance that your life is on track. And you can open yourself to small shifts you may need to make.

The beauty of introspection is not that it brings forward grand revelations but that it evokes a subtle, steady confidence and a trust built from within. This strong foundation will carry you through.

How lucky are you to have a front-row seat to your own life? You get to bear witness to your growth, healing, and evolution. Today, ask yourself how connected you are to your own story, and find time to soak up who you are, what you've accomplished, and all that is yet to be. Your life is worthy of this attention.

Remember, **allow yourself time and space to get to know yourself and honor who you are.**

SELF-LOVE SIMPLIFIED

Dear friend,

Loving and caring for yourself in this wild world can feel challenging and time-consuming. Sometimes we reduce *self-love* and *self-care* to things like drinking more green juice or drawing bubble baths (don't worry, I still love these things). But it's important that we don't stop at these surface-level practices.

Of course, sitcom binges and spa days make us feel good in the moment, but if we base our self-care solely on feel-good experiences like these, we might find that our happiness runs shallow. We risk missing out on true, meaningful love for ourselves.

Like so many things in life, self-love is a practice, a continual journey toward unapologetic self-acceptance. You might not achieve it overnight; it might take time to chip away at your own criticisms and doubts. But this is the work of going deeper to heal the relationship you have with yourself.

Real self-love requires a commitment to get to know yourself on an intimate level, so you can know how to better nourish and comfort your soul on a daily basis. Each small step you take toward building this relationship with yourself creates more space for you to love yourself and others.

Remember, **you are entitled to love as much as the people around you. Don't deny yourself the love you inherently deserve.**

FEBRUARY 9

FIND PEACE THROUGH INTENTION

Dear friend,

It's hard to decide what to do with our precious energy, isn't it? The world asks so much of us, and at times that can feel overwhelming. How can you recover a sense of calm and peace amid all the noise?

Setting intentions is the key to staying centered. With intentions, you can transform your mental state from unclear to clear, from confused to certain, from aimless to meaningful. When you tap into the true intentions for your life, you illuminate your path and unlock a new sense of purpose and clarity. Intentions help you know where to focus your energy and, conversely, where to let go.

Ask yourself today, *How do I intend to live? Where do I wish to place my energy, and in this moment, what matters most to me?* Notice the answers that rise to the surface before you have time to judge or fix them. These answers are clues to help you move forward into the life your heart craves and to live with intention.

Remember, intentions are the road maps to your life's journey. Find confidence and clarity with aligned intention.

ENDINGS AND BEGINNINGS

Dear friend,

One of the most beautiful aspects of the human existence is our ability to cultivate supportive, loving relationships. We get to experience the joy of having people in our corner who support us. This is the privilege of being seen, known, and understood.

Yet with all the wonderful experiences, memories, and emotions that come with relationships, they also bring heartbreak and pain. Life is filled with dualities.

Grieving the end of relationships is one of the hardest wounds to heal.

When I was going through a difficult breakup in my mid-twenties, I thought I would never get over the all-consuming heartache. At that time, my mom gifted me a bracelet with the words "This, too, shall pass" engraved on the inside. She hoped it would remind me that those difficult moments would eventually dissipate. I wore that bracelet every day for almost a year, allowing its words to inform my thinking and pull me out of my sadness. And it's true: No matter what challenges life is presenting to you today, you can breathe easy, knowing that everything is constantly changing, and this, too, will always pass.

Remember, **while nothing is permanent, every ending creates space in your life for a beautiful beginning.**

NAME YOUR FEELINGS

Dear friend,

When I was a child, my mom hung a felt poster on my wall that depicted common feelings. At the top of the page, it read: "How are you feeling today?" and we would regularly visit the poster and select a feeling for the day. This is one of my earliest memories of accessing my feelings without judgment. I could look at that poster, choose the emotion that felt most representative of my day, and not second-guess or place shame on it.

As I grew up, this practice with the poster faded away. I've judged my anger, resented my rage, and felt shame for my sadness. But even so, the memory of the poster has stuck with me; deep inside, I remember the freedom and ease that came with acknowledging and naming my feelings.

Getting in touch with your emotions, even when they feel challenging or uncomfortable, can teach you so much about yourself and what you really need. Difficult feelings can signify deep yearnings in your soul. When you pay attention to your emotional core, you can make the changes that will help you feel more centered and at peace.

So ask yourself, *How am I feeling today?*

Remember, **naming your feelings is a powerful practice of connection and self-awareness. It is safe to be present to what you feel.**

HONOR YOUR NEEDS

Dear friend,

Somewhere along my path, I picked up the idea that if I could become the most chill, low-maintenance, easygoing person, I would attain unfettered love and acceptance. I thought that *having* needs and being vocal about them translated into being *too needy*. I thought being needy would scare people away.

Trying to be need-less actually turned me into a shell of myself. And it makes sense. Human beings have needs, desires, and opinions. When those are stripped away, what do we have left?

It isn't admirable, attainable, or cool to live this way. What's cool is living with confidence, conviction, and self-assurance. Still, some people in your life will make you think you shouldn't express what you need and that, in doing so, you're inconvenient or too much.

Know that those people aren't for you. The people meant to be in your life will never shut you down, close you off, or make you feel bad for expressing who you are or what you want—they'll celebrate it. Your needs and wants are valid, and you're allowed to voice them and speak up for yourself.

Remember, **you don't have to apologize for your desires. Boldly stand up for who you are and what you need.**

IT'S NOT PERSONAL

Dear friend,

It's not easy being a sensitive soul in a harsh world. An area I've struggled with immensely is learning not to take everything that happens personally. It's utterly exhausting and disorienting when we're accustomed to internalizing the actions and behaviors of others. *Do we really have to live this way?*

Taking things personally can be subtle but insidious. Have you ever sensed a shift in energy from someone in your life and felt that you were to blame? Or maybe you overthink and overanalyze your thoughts and actions, seeking reassurance. Maybe you've even led yourself to think that if *you* could just be and do better, the *whole world* would be a better place. It's all too much, isn't it?

If you find yourself engaging in this vicious cycle, it's time to break it by seeking peace and acceptance. I promise, freedom and ease will come when you realize that you are not responsible for the words and actions of others.

Remember, **other people's behaviors are not a reflection of who you are. Find peace and comfort in yourself from within.**

LET LOVE IN

Dear friend,

Isn't it wonderful to love and be loved? The often harsh reality of human existence is eased by connection and care from others. We all desire relationships with people who support us, love us, and stand for us.

Painful scars from past events can subconsciously build walls around our hearts, guarding us from new experiences. I lived many years of my life closed off from others, despite my desire for love and companionship. I allowed the pain of my past to live on in the present. Ultimately, I was afraid of being hurt again, and I let that fear overtake my desire for connection. I subconsciously decided that love wasn't worth the risk.

Today, know that your past is not a predictor of your future. You are still so deserving of the love you desire. Don't let the people who were reckless with your heart close you off from those who will honor and care for it. Be open to the new; you are worthy of being loved and supported—always.

Remember, **love is worth the risk, and you are deserving of affection, kindness, and care.**

LISTEN AND LEARN

Dear friend,

As kids we're taught the importance of listening to others; as adults we know that listening is a sign of respect. But how often do we find ourselves truly listening—with intent and real presence? It feels like listening has become a lost art in our ever-evolving, transactional culture.

If you're feeling lonely and disconnected from the people in your life, actively listening can begin to bridge the gap. When you listen to what people say and take in the meaning of their words, you cultivate a deeper understanding and perspective. Through listening, you are able to release judgments of others and maybe even learn something new. Listening shows that you care, and it makes people feel valued and safe.

Do you want to transform your relationships and your life? Do you want to bring more ease, grace, and understanding into your interactions? Do you want to cultivate compassion and empathy in a world full of indifference and apathy? Lead with a listening ear, and stay open to the joy and connections that follow.

Remember, **when you choose to listen well, you create opportunities for genuine connection in your life.**

IT'S OKAY TO DISAGREE

Dear friend,

Disagreements are uncomfortable and anxiety producing. I grew up in an environment that was chaotic at times, filled with high emotions and heated tempers. As a child, I coped with these dynamics by seeking to be the peacekeeper. I thought that if I flew under the radar, didn't make too much noise, and never talked back, I could create peace.

I perceived disagreements as a signal that I was doing something wrong or that I hadn't worked hard enough to keep the peace. I thought confrontation was a sign of disrespect—an absence of love—but I had it all wrong. Disagreement is not inherently bad or unhealthy; it's *how* we disagree that matters most. Because each of us is unique, we're going to see the world from different points of view. What matters is that we learn to approach disagreement with calmness and acceptance, so we can use it as an opportunity to hear other people's beliefs and opinions.

Disagreeing with someone doesn't make you bad or wrong, and it doesn't mean you can't connect with that person from a place of love and understanding. Disagreement simply opens you to dialogue, to new perspectives, to a chance to learn.

Remember, having different opinions and beliefs is part of life. Continue to approach others with kindness, love, and compassion.

FEBRUARY 17

LET HOPE MOVE YOU

Dear friend,

If you're feeling overwhelmed by difficulty, remind yourself that no feeling will last forever. Everything in life is always changing, and this, too, shall pass.

When we make hope the cornerstone of our lives, there's nothing we can't do. It's what inspires us to break unhealthy family cycles, seek help when we need it, and confidently forge our own paths.

Hope asks you to expand your imagination and invites you to focus on how good the world *could* be rather than what it currently is. Having hope lifts you up, moving you forward when you feel scared or sad, because you believe there's more good to be had.

Whatever personal dark storm you may be facing, seek to be gentle, loving, and kind with yourself. Latch on to optimism for what is to come. Know that you won't feel this way forever. The storm will one day lift, and when it does, you will still be standing, ready to claim a brighter day. Lean on the hope within you for fuel to get you through this moment. Light is on the way.

Remember, **the troubles of today will eventually be memories. Take heart in knowing that life will always evolve.**

JUMP-START CHANGE

Dear friend,

Sometimes life makes it crystal clear that we need a change. We've noticed the signs, felt the pull; it's time to pivot. Acknowledging necessary change is always the first step. But what happens when we know we need to make a move but aren't quite sure what that looks like?

Discomfort and fear of the unknown can paralyze the decision-making process. Relax and remember: You don't have to make all your changes at once.

If you're being called in a new direction but aren't sure where to go first, open yourself up to small, simple changes in your daily routine. Mix up your regular life and become familiar with new environments. Get creative and think outside the box, following small sparks of inspiration and excitement.

Trust the confidence you have within you, and remember that you don't have to do everything perfectly; you can (and will) make mistakes along the way. That means you have permission to start before you feel ready, just one little bit at a time.

Remember, **don't let your fear hold you back from making a change and becoming who you are yearning to be.**

ACCEPT LIFE'S LITTLE NUDGES

Dear friend,

Your life is one of a kind, and your uniqueness is a gift. No one will ever live the life you're living, and you have a purpose that's specific to you. As exciting as this is, perhaps your uniqueness can sometimes make you feel isolated. What do you do when you feel like no one understands?

When I feel like I'm walking the path of life alone, I take solace in one simple but powerful practice: trusting that I am always being guided. By what, you ask? I'm not sure, to be honest. Give it a name that resonates with you.

I take comfort in knowing that there's a gentle presence outside of me that's helping me maneuver through life. You can too. When you set a goal or endeavor to create something important in this world and you feel the need for additional support, look for those subtle winks and quiet nudges that confirm you are on the right path.

You have everything you need, and you are never walking through life alone.

Remember, **when you feel lost, tune in to the signs that are guiding you and accept life's little nudges. Let your life lead you.**

CELEBRATE YOUR WINS

Dear friend,

Do you ever feel as though your efforts have gone unnoticed and that maybe it's not in the cards for you to experience the success, validation, and gratification of big goals being reached?

If you answered yes, this is why it's important to celebrate tiny wins along the way. When you are so laser-focused on the big picture, it's easy to lose sight of the small, incremental steps that, in reality, are monumental in your journey. Each move you make toward what you desire is something to commemorate, because pursuing your dreams is an act of bravery in a world filled with doubt and criticism.

Let the big goals and aspirations you hold for your life guide you through each day, and envision what it will feel like to reach the finish line. But keep in mind, we never know when, if, or how our dreams will unfold. So be present to the steps you take along the way, and know that you are always in action and en route to all you desire. Those small achievements deserve your honor and praise. Celebrate a tiny win today.

Remember, **each day that you are alive, you are accomplishing something. Give yourself credit!**

FEBRUARY 20

LET YOURSELF BE DIFFERENT

Dear friend,

Deep down, we all want to belong. When we feel like we don't have a safe space, being different hurts even more. I tried for so long to fit in and be like everyone else. I wanted to fit the mold and have the right hair, the right clothes, the right vibe. I tried to cultivate acceptance in all the wrong places.

I never accomplished this goal of fitting in, though. And by doing everything I could to make others like me, I veered farther and farther away from who I truly was.

It wasn't worth it. No matter if we're young or old, the pressure to belong will always linger. But as we get to know ourselves better and discover who we really are, we can combat this pressure and welcome the blessing of allowing ourselves to be different and wonderfully unique.

You don't have to spend time changing in order to fit in. Confidently embrace who you are, knowing that your unique qualities are what others love about you. Today, celebrate what makes you *you*.

Remember, there is only one *you* in this world. Don't spend your energy trying to mold yourself to be like someone else.

EACH DAY IS A GIFT

Dear friend,

If you're reading this, you woke up this morning and received an amazing gift: a brand-new day. How incredible that you get to decide what to do with it!

The truth is, we don't know when our time will be up in this life, so we should ask ourselves, *What can I do today to live life to the fullest, with gratitude and presence?*

I learned this lesson in an intense way when my dad passed away unexpectedly in his sleep when I was twenty-one years old. I, of course, was devastated by this loss, and I became consumed with the unpredictable nature of life and how, without notice, it can be cut short. This deeply painful chapter proved to be one of my life's biggest teachers; it was a powerful reminder to cherish each day and not take life for granted.

I share this story to encourage you to remember the blessing of every moment in life. It's easy to fall into complacency and frustration. But your mind is powerful, and you can shift your perspective through gratitude and presence. What are you grateful for, and what will you bring to today?

Remember, **your life is a blessing—to you and to everyone around you. Hold gratitude for your presence in this world.**

THE LIMITS OF CLOSURE

Dear friend,

Are you looking for closure in a difficult situation? I want to let you off the hook. I want you to feel freedom from a past event that has a grip on you in the present.

For so much of my life, I believed I had to know the *why*s behind difficult situations. Searching for closure, I thought I had to have all the answers to move forward.

As we know, sometimes we don't get those answers.

Reflection is an important part of healing, but if you find yourself consumed with asking about the *why*s of your past, you can inhibit your growth and keep yourself stuck. The search for *why*, when taken to an extreme, can keep you from your peace.

The hard truth is that sometimes you won't get the closure you seek. Sometimes you won't know all the answers or find life's circumstances tied up with a bow. But the silver lining to this truth is that you can still move forward. You can find peace without closure; you can find freedom in the present.

Remember, you're allowed to create closure for your life and release the need to know all the answers. Move forward with peace.

YOU ARE INTUITIVE

Dear friend,

I've been captivated by the concept of *intuition* for years. Intuition tends to feel elusive and mysterious, like some sort of all-knowing aspect of ourselves that pops up in our lives to guide us.

I used to think I was excluded from the intuitive life, born without that inner knowing. The truth is, I have intuition; I was just ignoring it. This was part of my lack of connection with myself. As soon as I started intentionally rebuilding that connection, my intuition fell back into place.

I want you to know that you have this gift too; you are intuitive. Your inner voice, which helps you maneuver through the winding roads of life, won't betray you. The trick is learning to listen to it and trust it. Following your intuition has the potential to show you a life better than what you could have imagined and to open doors you thought were sealed shut. Today, spend some time connecting with your intuition. Don't judge or criticize what you hear; be curious, open, and receptive.

Remember, **your intuition is strong and always within you, waiting for you to tune in.**

FEBRUARY 25

WHAT REAL POSITIVITY LOOKS LIKE

Dear friend,

You're probably familiar with the "good vibes only" ethos in our culture. It almost makes us fear negativity and believe we should have positive thoughts *only*, eliminating anything deemed too pessimistic. This is where I think we get it wrong. It's simply not possible to live this way.

Avoiding the negative and uncomfortable for the sake of attaining perfect positivity is what we call *toxic positivity*. Doesn't sound good, does it? I'm sure you've experienced it at some point—that false, forced happiness, with a sense of discontent brewing beneath the surface.

So how can we embrace true, healthy positivity? For me, it's through understanding that life contains highs and lows. It's by being honest with myself and being truthful with others. It's by acknowledging when things are hard and accepting the heavy thoughts rather than pushing them to the side.

With this kind of honesty and adaptability, you can develop true confidence and *real* positivity, because you know you can handle what comes at you. Today, choose to nurture that kind of positivity within yourself.

Remember, there is magic in the good, the bad, and everything in between.

BE BRAVE EVERY DAY

Dear friend,

Perhaps we think bravery is a trait set aside for soldiers, superheroes, and risk-takers—not for those of us with seemingly mundane, ordinary lives. Because of this perception, we might overlook the role of bravery in our own stories.

Today, reimagine bravery in a way that fits you. Release the tendency to pigeonhole bravery into those rare, monumental, dramatic acts of courage so few of us identify with. The truth is, you can be brave every single day. Being exactly who you are is brave. Showing up honestly in a world that consistently asks you to edit yourself is brave. Being loving and kind and accepting is brave. Pursuing your dreams is brave.

Do these definitions resonate with you?

We can all practice bravery every day in small but meaningful ways. Consider the moments when you displayed bravery yesterday—what did you do? Can you repeat those actions today? Be proud of the way bravery shows up in your life in quiet, everyday examples.

Remember, **stepping into your life with self-trust and confidence is an act of bravery.**

HOW DO YOU CARE FOR *YOU*?

Dear friend,

What have you done for *you* lately? As your friend, I'm offering you this gentle nudge to remind you to take good care of yourself on a regular basis. This is part of becoming your own best friend—learning how to intuitively care for yourself.

We are so accustomed to overextending ourselves and caring for others, but rarely do we take the time to ask ourselves what *we* need, day in and day out.

How you care for yourself is unique to your own needs. When I'm overstimulated, I find comfort in solitude. When I'm sad, my favorite sitcom soothes me. When I'm confused, I get out in nature and restore myself.

What works for you?

Take time today to do at least one thing that leaves you feeling revitalized. Something as simple as ordering from a favorite restaurant or spending ten minutes in a quiet place may be all you need. Let me remind you that you are worthy of care and compassion, and you never need an explanation for prioritizing your well-being.

Remember, **care for yourself today like you would care for a dear friend. You deserve it.**

IT'S OKAY TO BE ANNOYED

Dear friend,

Do you ever have those days when everything and everyone utterly annoys you? I've been known to have an irritable side (we can't all be perfect!). My moodiness, when unchecked, really spirals into an unpleasant version of myself. And, as you might guess, when I feed my moods with enabling thoughts, I become a total mess.

When I was a kid, my mom would try to lift me out of my irritability. She knew that awareness and acknowledgment led to resolution. When I was annoyed, she'd ask, "What are you down on today?" I would be down on friends, down on family, down on school, and naming my annoyance often released me from the feelings of it.

I share this with you to remind you that all feelings are valid, even your irritability. It's what you do with these feelings, how you act on them and manage them, that matters most. So whenever you get annoyed, today or in the future, think of me and my mom and ask yourself, *What am I down on today?* It might give you a laugh and help you move forward in peace.

Remember, **it's okay to have complicated feelings in a messy world. Be gentle with yourself.**

FEBRUARY 29

EMBRACE YOUR LIFE

Dear friend,

Have you ever found yourself wishing you had someone else's life? We can waste so much of our time yearning for something else (or yearning to be someone else), denying the beauty of our unique existence. It's natural to fall into the "grass is greener" mentality, but when you do, you miss out on the magnificence of your life and rob yourself of true fulfillment.

Rather than wishing for things to be different, how can you seek to lovingly accept who you are, imperfections and all? Ask yourself, *How would I feel if I unapologetically loved and trusted my life, my path, and my journey?* Comparing yourself will only add to your pain and suffering. Stop resisting your reality and engage with it instead. When you commit to embracing your journey—your challenges, mistakes, and flaws included—you will be presented with a deep sense of inner peace.

Give yourself permission to be a champion of your own life and take full ownership—every part of it.

―――――

Remember, **there is only one *you*. Your life is precious, and you cannot mess it up.**

MARCH 1

FIND YOUR FOCUS

Dear friend,

I'll confess: Writing this love note to you felt hard today because so many temptations were grabbing at my attention. It's not always easy to focus! Our culture often glorifies our ability to multitask. But I ask you: How do you feel when your attention is divided and your presence is diminished? I ask this with absolutely no judgment; as I said, it's something I struggle with too. Multitasking makes me feel scattered and overwhelmed, and I find I'm *less* productive when I try to accomplish too many things at once. Does that resonate with you? If it does, can I ask you to try something?

Experiment with staying in the present moment, limiting your attention to one thing at a time. With a singular focus, we often feel more productive, connected, and fulfilled. We become more aware of life's small joys and can better exhibit love and kindness toward others because we are fully able to show up for them.

Today, be present and take one task at a time. The practice of presence is always worthwhile.

Remember, **you choose where to place your focus; stay present from moment to moment.**

YOU DESERVE HAPPINESS

Dear friend,

When I think of happiness, I think of childlike joy, freedom and fun, and contentment and trust in what is. Happiness, for me, feels like a deep sigh of relief that all is well in the present moment. As we get older, the harshness of the world can convince us that authentic happiness isn't possible. That life is too hard for it. But why can't difficulty and happiness coexist?

Life is challenging, but that doesn't mean happiness can't shine through. Happiness isn't dependent on your circumstances; it's a product of your relationship with yourself. It's the result of self-love and self-respect cultivated over time. It builds from a steady practice of contentment as you train yourself to look for the magic all around you, trusting it's always there.

Happiness is your right.

When you prioritize knowing yourself, when you trust the unique path of your life, happiness will make its way to you. Today, let go of the expectations, attachments, and disappointments convincing you that you can't be happy. Practice gratitude and contentment, and remind yourself that happiness is available to you when you're open to it.

Remember, **you are allowed to be happy, despite what's happening around you. Be open to the peace and contentment your soul desires.**

MARCH 3

RECOGNIZE LABELS

Dear friend,

Who are you? When faced with this existential question—with limitless answers—you might rely on surface-level labels: You're someone's child, friend, parent. You're an employee or a student. You're a banker, a writer, an artist. These labels describe your roles in life, but do they accurately depict the totality of who you are?

I remember a time in my life when this question terrified me. I felt mounting pressure to answer in a way that others would accept and understand. Sometimes I would even edit how I labeled myself, changing like a chameleon, to fit into specific places with specific people. I rarely stopped to ask what the true answer to this question was.

No matter how you describe yourself to others (or how others describe you), ultimately, *you* get to decide how to define the core of your existence. With the intention of being true to the real you, how would you describe who you are in this world? If you could release others' expectations of you, who would you be?

Look out for labels, and choose only the ones that truly fit you. You are free to be who you want to be—isn't that wonderful?

Remember, **no one has the power to name who you are. This is your birthright. You get to write your story.**

ADD TO YOUR CONFIDENCE

Dear friend,

The relationship you have with yourself can feel constantly in flux. One day you feel like you have it all together, and in a split second, everything changes. Small moments rock your world, and unexpected changes shake your perceptions of life. You are left questioning everything, feeling assured of nothing.

Confidence is crafted over time, through personal connection and practiced resilience. Life will throw curveballs in your path, but if you stay open and curious, those curveballs can become gateways to a new level of awareness and knowledge.

So what can you do to strengthen your confidence in this journey of life?

Release the relationships that harm your mental health, the ones that make you feel small or less-than. Take tiny steps toward your goals and dreams, and every time you follow through, your assuredness and trust in yourself will increase. Become aware of how you talk to yourself and consciously speak to yourself just like you would to a loved one. You can become your own biggest cheerleader.

Believe in your ability to fortify yourself today, despite what the world puts in your path.

Remember, **you are stronger and more capable than you give yourself credit for.**

MARCH 4

MINIMIZE MISUNDERSTANDING

Dear friend,

Many of the misunderstandings and arguments in my life have stemmed from miscommunication. This usually happens when I'm afraid of saying what I really want to say or when I hastily speak from fleeting emotions. Can you relate?

How we manage our relationships directly correlates to our sense of peace. Our people matter deeply to us, and these loving and caring relationships are central to our joy—which is why it's so painful when crossed wires and communication mishaps create disconnect. How can the relationships that bring us joy also breed so much angst?

It's important to communicate with one another in a clear, kind way. Convey how you feel and simultaneously consider the impact of your words; speak your truth but also be present to how your words land. Clarity in communication stems from confidence in your perspective and kindness in your intent.

Today, give yourself permission to speak up, to communicate your needs, and to be caring with your words so you can be heard and understood.

Remember, **your truth and your feelings are worthy of expression. Find freedom through clear and kind communication.**

FIND POWER IN CHOICE

Dear friend,

Have you ever witnessed two indecisive people trying to figure out where to eat? The back-and-forth of "I don't care" and "whatever you want" can be one of the most irritating social dynamics. Why is it so grinding to be faced with indecision?

Life is filled with opportunities to choose, and that can lead to decision fatigue and indifference. But does it really benefit us to give away our power of choice?

Your ability to choose is your power, and every choice you make is an opportunity to vocalize your desire. Indecision chips away at your confidence, clarity, and self-worth. It leads to a stifling of your longings and a denial of what you really want.

Today, find empowerment in your daily decisions. Each time you are asked to choose is an opportunity to choose yourself. And every time you make a choice, you strengthen your relationship with yourself and build self-trust. Listen to and trust your soul's desires, and give yourself the power to choose with confidence.

Remember, **when you're not sure what to choose, look within for the answer.**

TAKE SPACE

MARCH 7

Dear friend,

I want to let you in on a little secret about me; we are friends, after all! Despite many years of inner work, I can be quite feisty when pushed to my limits. I've been known to relish snarky comebacks in challenging situations, and I've often succumbed to knee-jerk reactions and impulses, letting myself say whatever comes to mind without thinking of the consequences.

As you can imagine, I have said things that were hurtful and untrue in the heat of the moment, which has led to remorse and unnecessary stress. After cleaning up one too many messes from this habit, I came to a life-changing realization: Not every situation requires an immediate reaction.

Instead, you can take space to decide the best course of action. You can pause, breathe, collect yourself. Then, once you've moved through your feelings, you can refocus and consider how you want to proceed in the conversation. If you find yourself in a tense moment today, take space and find power in the pause.

Remember, **when feeling pressured to respond, give yourself space to pause, breathe, and decide.**

BEING, NOT DOING

Dear friend,

As goal-seekers and dream-makers, we have high aspirations for how we want life to pan out. We often ask ourselves, *What do I need to do to get where I want to be?* We are hardwired to focus on the action, on the doing. Our culture values productivity, after all!

When I was young, my mom pointed this out to me: We are human *beings*, not human *doings*. This simple shift in perspective changed how I approach life, guiding me in how to tackle change, decision, and uncertainty. Now when I'm at a crossroads or simply feeling off course, I remember I'm a *being*, not a *doing*. So let me ask you:

> What energy are you living in right now?
> Are you stuck in fear?
> Are you living freely?
> Are you joyful?

Think of the qualities you wish to bring forward in your life and notice whether your current energy matches your desires. Is there somewhere you could shift from *doing* to *being*? One of the benefits of *being* and reflecting on yourself is understanding how you want to feel and allowing your energy to meet that feeling. Then you find yourself closer to where you want to be.

Remember, **you are a human *being*. Your energy and your presence speak for you.**

BEAUTY IN YOUR FLAWS

Dear friend,

    I like to think that each of our lives is a work of art. Each story is a masterpiece: unique, abstract, and personal. As the artists of our lives, it's normal to want to create something beautiful and perfect. But do we allow space for errors and mistakes? Or do we assume flaws will ruin it all?

    We are multifaceted human beings, doing our best to make it through life. We will make painful mistakes, and we believe those mistakes make us unworthy. Know that the messiness and missteps add to your art rather than detract from it.

    Seek to release the fear of messing up the creative canvas of your life. Any errors made along the way will only provide depth and meaning. Your mistakes give you experience, wisdom, and unexpected opportunities to grow. So today, find beauty in the humbling instances you once viewed as flaws, knowing that every moment adds to the masterpiece of you.

Remember, **be grateful for your mistakes and the lessons they have provided. You wouldn't be who you are today without them.**

LET PATIENCE BE YOUR GUIDE

MARCH 10

Dear friend,

I'm a patient person when it comes to the small stuff of life. I'm not usually bothered by traffic or long lines. I'm not generally agitated by the slow pace of a regular day. Patience comes easily to me in these instances.

But I do tend to be impatient about the pace at which my life unfolds. If I have a desire or a dream, I want it *now*, and that impatience breeds discontent. Though it's natural to feel excited for the future, how can we embody patience while we await the dreams we desire?

Being patient on your path means being present to each moment and remembering that the steps you take in your life while on your way to the goal are just as important as the destination itself. When you are patient with your timelines, you aren't wishing time away, hoping you'll arrive faster; you feel grateful for the right here, right now.

Can you find peace today, knowing you've done your part and life will work out for you? Breathe in a sigh of relief, trusting your time will come.

Remember, **develop the practice of waiting; your patience is an invaluable strength.**

UNEARTH AUTHENTICITY

Dear friend,

The word *authenticity* is commonly thrown around as a virtue to attain or an ideal to strive for, as if it's a quality that lives somewhere outside of ourselves. But what if your authentic self is already there, waiting for you to uncover it?

Many of us have spent years bending and molding ourselves to fit in, sometimes to the point that we almost can't recognize who we really are and what we really want. If that feels true for you, then be encouraged that, today, the authentic version of you is still buried deep inside.

If you've been living according to the expectations and standards of the external, making the switch to authentic living will likely stir up feelings of fear and doubt. But if you are willing to work through that fear, you will experience your most natural, authentic self.

When you uncover this version of you, you will never want to bury it again. That is the power of living authentically.

Remember, **your uniqueness is a gift; don't rob the world of who you truly are.**

DON'T LOSE YOUR WONDER

Dear friend,

Did you daydream as a child? What visions did you create when your imagination was permitted to run wild, back when you had ample time and before the influence of others got in the way?

There's something precious and powerful about childlike wonder. Maybe it's the unfiltered desire or the lack of doubt and self-judgment. I often consider how life might feel if I lived this way from childhood, uninterrupted, into adulthood and to the present day.

In my experience, imagination is the pathway to so much goodness and joy. Creativity, optimism, and hope stem from the imagination. When we cannot see the outcomes we long for in our physical realities, our minds can take us where we want to go. Our imaginations can keep us motivated to stay the course of what we truly want.

Today, ask yourself, *When was the last time I carved out space to let my mind wander and imagine what could be?* Let go of judgment and productivity, and rekindle that childlike curiosity as you let your imagination run wild.

Remember, **you're allowed to dream, to imagine, to wonder. Be creative with your life.**

MARCH 12

MARCH 13

THE POWER OF SOLITUDE

Dear friend,

How often do you *choose* to spend time in your own company? For many of us, being alone brings forth complicated emotions and critical thoughts. You might have grown up with the perception that being alone is a symptom of flaws or unlikability, that it means you aren't worthy of company. In reality, there is power, purpose, and meaning in solitude.

Quality time spent with yourself breeds connection and imaginative breakthroughs. You can discover so much about who you are in the silence of your own company. When you learn to love your own presence and bask in your solitude, you can access newfound confidence, independence, and empowerment.

Restoration and revitalization come in abundance when we are alone. Solitude allows us to be focused, present, and introspective. What could you experience if you took the time to be with yourself? What could you discover or heal? How could you grow or change? The time you spend *on* yourself, *by* yourself, is never wasted and will always be worthwhile.

Remember, **when you love your own company, you are never truly alone; find power in your own presence today.**

UNCLUTTER YOUR LIFE

Dear friend,

Have you ever stepped into a cluttered room and immediately felt overwhelmed? Things chaotically strewn everywhere, no rhyme or reason—just madness. Clutter can make us feel out of sorts, anxious, and out of control.

Like physical clutter, emotional clutter can also feel draining and disorienting. Think of how much you take in mentally every day. You are constantly fielding emotions, opinions, mindsets, and judgments. It's a lot to process, and it's easy for everything to pile up within you. When I sense this happening to me, I take it as a sign to pause and evaluate what's happening in my life and what feels like too much.

If you're feeling like your emotions are piling up, you can unclutter what you're taking in and release what isn't in your best interest. Do you need to take a break? Reconnect? Process your emotions? Sometimes our inner lives get cluttered because we're afraid to let go and clear things out. Yet letting go creates space for clarity, opportunity, and new energy.

Take time to consider what's happening in just one emotional corner of your life and try some mental spring cleaning today.

Remember, **you're allowed to let go of the people, places, and things that no longer align with your ideals.**

MARCH 14

DO YOU KNOW YOU?

Dear friend,

One of my favorite authors, James Finley, once said, "Could you live your whole life never having met the person who is living it?"[1] This idea was the wake-up call I needed, because it described the life that I had been living.

I didn't know myself. But the day I read this, it felt like I had been given permission to *want* to know myself, and it set me on my journey to self-realization and self-love.

Being in constant connection and conversation with my true self has become my top priority in life. This has allowed me to know who I am and what I want, and it has given me the clarity and answers that used to feel so far away from me. It has instilled in me an unshakable confidence that my place in this world matters.

Let today be the day you recommit yourself to the loving journey of knowing exactly who you are, with excitement and curious optimism for what you will find along the way. How wonderful is it to be you? How amazing is it to witness your life? What a privilege to know and love yourself fully!

Remember, no one in this world is like you; you are one of one. Don't let the magic of who you are pass you by.

MANIFESTATION THROUGH VISUALIZATION

Dear friend,

The time between the first spark of a desire and seeing that desire come to fruition can sometimes feel endless. We start to question whether it's really meant to be, creating an anxiety-producing waiting game. We torture ourselves with overthinking and uncertainty.

Or we can make a different choice. The thing is, we don't have to wait for our dreams to come true to *feel* what we desire. We don't have to waste our time waiting for particular outcomes, because the present moment is always where we have the greatest opportunity to influence our future.

One of my favorite practices for connecting my desires of the present to the outcomes of the future is visualization. In allowing yourself to see the person you want to be and feel how you want to feel, you build excitement for what's to come. This excitement propels you forward on those in-between days when you start to doubt yourself.

When you envision what you want for your life, can you let tomorrow's success fuel today's joy? Excitement and optimism will come through visualizing your goals and anticipating that they will become a reality.

Remember, **the desires you have for your life can be felt now. Don't deny yourself the feeling of success just because you haven't yet met the goal.**

FLIP THE SCRIPT

Dear friend,

Think about it: You are the only person who lives with you twenty-four hours a day. While this might feel daunting, it's actually pretty cool. You are the witness to your own life, so why not do everything you can to foster and deepen the connection you have with yourself?

Your life is narrated by a constant stream of your own thoughts. Tune in to your inner conversation today. Is the script of your life pessimistic? Or do your thoughts support and nurture you? Many of us live in a repetitive loop of negativity. So ask yourself, *Is the kind of narration I'm experiencing what I want for the story of my life?* Take stock of what you repeat to yourself daily. Seek moments in your day when you can replace unnecessary worry with assuredness.

My go-to practice for flipping the script is repeating affirmations like "All is well in this moment." Try it out, or come up with a phrase that feels loving and nourishing to you. With this mindful presence, you remember the power you hold within, the power to flip the script at any time.

Remember, there's much you cannot control, but you *can* manage the narrative you craft within yourself.

CULTIVATE REAL ACCEPTANCE

Dear friend,

    Whenever I think about the topic of acceptance, this quote from Eckhart Tolle comes to mind: "Accept—then act. Whatever the present moment contains, accept it as if you had chosen it. Always work with it, not against it. Make it your friend and ally, not your enemy. This will miraculously transform your whole life."[2]

    When I first heard this quote, I was stuck in a web of confusion, anger, and denial over my life's circumstances. The idea of working *with* the moment was simply revolutionary.

    Accepting where you are is not an act of giving up or letting go. It's not condoning or making judgments on your life. It's standing firmly in the present, grounded in your reality, knowing that in this moment you have a choice, and your choice has power.

    So many of us shy away from accepting reality because we don't like what we're facing, and that's a completely natural reaction. But today, if you find yourself in a moment of resistance to what is, try working *with* what's happening. Release the habit of judging your reality and lean in to acceptance, knowing that you are powerful enough to move your way through.

Remember, **you may not have the power to change the moment in front of you, but you do have the power to choose to accept it.**

HOW'S IT GOING BEING YOU TODAY?

Dear friend,

When people ask me how I'm doing, I usually respond on autopilot with an "I'm good!" without checking in with myself. To change it up, my mom has started asking me, "How's it going being you today?" This subtle but powerful change in the question created space for me to tune in to myself and understand how I am feeling, from moment to moment. I'm grateful for my mom, who always finds fun ways to weave mindfulness into regular life.

So now I ask you: How's it going being you today? How's it going living your life? How does it feel to be you in this world? These seemingly simple questions have the potential to transform the relationship you have with yourself and offer access to a deeper knowledge of who you are and what you want.

A connected and centered life will require constant conversation with yourself. Questions like these nudge you to reflect on your day-to-day progress, to see whether the choices you're making will help you reach the intentions you've set for yourself.

Remember, in taking time to ask yourself important questions, you live a life of purpose.

BUILD MEANING IN SMALL MOMENTS

Dear friend,

When I was younger, I prioritized *maximalism* in all aspects of the word. I thought I had to have more, be more, experience more, earn more. The more, the better—always.

This lifestyle fueled the belief that nothing I had was ever good enough. I always had to be working, dreaming, and looking toward the next goal or accomplishment. As you can imagine, this pattern never produced happiness or fulfillment, just a hamster-wheel mentality with no off-ramp.

Rather than seeking more, I needed to do less. I learned that simplicity, intention, and mindfulness are far more powerful than meaningless excess. When we embrace simplicity, we realize the true abundance of our current reality. Meaning, success, and purpose aren't confined to big moments of achievement; they can also be found in the small, overlooked in-betweens.

Today, seek to find the meaning of your life's simple moments. Embrace the mundane, the ordinary. In doing so, you'll expand your mindset to the magic of all aspects of your existence.

Remember, so much joy can be found in the everyday moments of life. Allow yourself the space to feel that joy and be grateful for it.

YOU ARE LOVABLE

Dear friend,

Here's an uncomfortable truth: People in your life will try to make you feel that you aren't worthy of love and affection. But here's a little secret: Those people are not your people.

If someone from your past has planted a seed in your mind that who you are isn't worthy of kindness or care, or that you're not easy to love, let today be the day that you know deep in your heart it's just not true.

Think of relationships as trial and error. When you meet someone, you can't predict how the relationship will unfold. You simply show up and hope for the best. Inevitably, some people will come into your life and rock your spirit and make you question the core of who you are. Again, those aren't your people.

Today, breathe in all the love that you know you are worthy of, and breathe out the past that ever made you think otherwise. Give yourself permission to let go of anyone who tried to take away your birthright of caring human connection. Affirm to yourself that you are worthy, lovable, and always enough, and really let yourself believe it.

Remember, **you are innately worthy of love and connection; nothing you say or do will ever take away from that.**

BECOMING THE LUCKY ONE

Dear friend,

Have you ever wished you could be one of the "lucky" ones? Those people who seemingly have everything work out and who make life look easy? We often spend so much time yearning for a smoother path. But as we know, we can't will ourselves into a new life. I am who I am; you are who you are. So how can we work with that rather than against it?

What's cool is that you can start to live like the lucky ones right now. Your thoughts are powerful, and they shape your perceived reality. How can you consciously curate your thoughts to produce a more harmonious lived experience?

Notice the patterns in your mind and tune in to how they make you feel. Narrow down the thoughts that go against what you wish to create. You'll find glimmers of relief when you change the way you think. Believing in yourself and your abilities will propel you forward.

What do you want to create today? Who do you want to be? It starts in your mind.

Remember, **your thoughts are powerful and influence your reality; choose wisely.**

MARCH 22

THE REAL MEANING OF LIFE

Dear friend,

At some point we all ponder those big existential questions: *What is the meaning of life? Why am I here?* I won't pretend to be a philosopher or an authority on how you might answer these questions for yourself, but as I've considered them for my own life, I've come up with some musings that give me great comfort and understanding. Rather than feeling overwhelmed by questions about the world, I find peace by narrowing my focus to *my* role within it.

The meaning of my life, I've determined, is to know and love exactly who I am. To be connected to myself and understand my deserved place in this world—to be certain that I matter. My meaning comes from unapologetically being myself and using my gifts with intention. That's what I've come up with.

What feels right for you? What comes up when you ask yourself these questions? Do you find relief in knowing that your meaning is unique to you? You can respond to these questions in your own time and space, acknowledging that your answers may shift and grow as you do.

Remember, we all are here for a reason and have a unique purpose in this world. We all matter, and we all belong.

HOW DO PEOPLE MAKE YOU FEEL?

Dear friend,

In relationships, I used to have an "I'll take whatever I can get" mentality. I never wanted to be alone, so I made myself believe I could make any relationship work. I was a master at adjusting myself and blending in, and it never occurred to me to consider how the people around me actually made me feel.

I lived for years collecting people but never questioning whether they were healthy for me. As you can imagine, this ultimately led to a collapse of my social circle. I painfully learned that the cliché is true: *It's about quality, not quantity.* Relationships are no different. Now I'd rather be completely alone than feel lonely surrounded by people who make me feel like I'm not appreciated.

How do the people in your life make you feel? Do you feel seen? Honored? Respected? Understood? Included? Use these feelings to guide you in deciding who is meant to be in your circle. Know that to be in your presence is a gift; you are a prize.

Remember, **you deserve to be treated with kindness, care, and compassion. Don't settle for anything less.**

MAKE TIME FOR WHAT MATTERS

Dear friend,

I've been teaching meditation and mindfulness classes and workshops with my mom for more than a decade. It's such a privilege to witness people making their mental health and well-being a priority and to help them incorporate these practices in their lives.

Without a doubt, though, the most common hindrance I hear that keeps people from committing to their practices is time. Everyone feels like they don't have enough time to add one more task into their schedules. Their plates are already full. It's true—the pressure of responsibility builds up fast. It can feel impossible to even consider adding more to your life, but today I want to give you permission to create space, wherever you can find it.

So often we think we need enormous amounts of time to make well-being a priority. But that's not true. If you dedicate even a few moments of your day to connection, contemplation, and inspiration, you will soon experience their benefits. This could mean taking a minute with yourself before you grab your phone first thing in the morning or spending a few moments in your car to breathe deeply before heading into work. These small acts of mindfulness may not seem like much, but they matter.

Remember, **create space in your day to nourish yourself; it's always worthwhile.**

IN COMMUNITY

Dear friend,

If you're reading this letter, you're probably interested in living your best life. You care about the energy you put out in the world, and you desire to feel purposeful and loved. You're dedicated to living your life with intention, and I think you're amazing!

Often, when we embark on a personal development journey, we become immersed in ourselves. It's natural; we want to be better, so we spend a lot of time in introspection. Yet equally important to our growth is the support of a loving community, which has an immeasurable impact on who we become.

Today, I want to remind you of how beneficial and necessary it is to have supportive people in your corner who will cheer for you and lift you up when you need it most. Plus, when you work together with people who share your values, you can achieve real change.

Don't deprive your life of the beauty of community. Seek out the people who share your ideals and values and who you can enjoy life with. You deserve to feel that love and support.

Remember, **you are not meant to walk your path alone. You deserve to feel kindness, care, and support from the people in your life.**

MARCH 27

TAKE OWNERSHIP OF YOUR LIFE

Dear friend,

One of the most powerful traits we can cultivate is taking ownership of and responsibility for our thoughts, words, and actions. For me, this has been a game changer.

There's power in acknowledging that the only person truly responsible for your actions is you. While sometimes we might wish we could pass off responsibility or blame, we find a deep-seated confidence and power when we own our choices and hold ourselves accountable for the things we say and do.

Denying ownership of your actions only disconnects you from yourself. Being responsible and accountable for what you do allows you to feel aligned with your purpose and at peace with reality. It's empowering to look at it this way, isn't it?

Today, lean in to the power you can feel when you know that everything you say and do has purpose and aligns with your integrity. Uncover the self-trust that comes when you live from this place of ownership.

———

Remember, you are in charge of your life. Embrace your path, own your choices, and feel pride for who you are.

RETHINK PRODUCTIVITY

MARCH 28

Dear friend,

You are more than what you accomplish in this life, and you mean more than your productivity. Whether you hear it regularly or not, I hope you know how much people value and appreciate exactly who you are, not just what you do.

Our days are often structured around efficiency; others are counting on us to show up at optimal performance to complete long, complicated task lists. On top of these external pressures, we have internal pressures to feel like we are making a substantive difference in our homes, communities, and workplaces. We want to believe our lives matter.

Take a breath and remind yourself that you are not on this planet to simply produce. You are creative and magical, and your contributions are important—but you also need rest and restoration. Give yourself permission not to get everything done today, and know that time set aside for yourself is important and necessary too. Personal time solidifies the strong foundation you have within to shine as bright as you can.

Remember, **giving yourself the gift of time and space breeds creativity. You're allowed to take a break.**

YOU DON'T HAVE TO BE THE FIXER

Dear friend,

I recently learned about the psychological concept of *emotional monitoring*. It's subconsciously feeling the need to control and manage the moods of people around you to maintain peace and avoid conflict.[3] When I learned that there is a name for the pattern I embodied for many years, I felt so much relief.

Growing up in toxic dynamics, I became an expert at anticipating others' problems and did my best to mitigate conflict when I could. I thought that if I was "on" enough, then I could be the one to create peace—to fix it.

This led me to becoming the unofficial PR agent for the difficult people in my life. I would make excuses and attempt to mitigate others' disrespectful words, all to prevent uncomfortable moments. I gave people passes for their bad behavior by often being the one to clean up the messes they had made.

If you resonate with being the fixer for the people in your life, I invite you to let go of this habit. You are not responsible for maintaining someone else's peace. Today, you can give a rest to emotional monitoring and refocus on your well-being.

Remember, you are not responsible for the words or actions of the people around you. Release yourself from this role and regain your peace.

DROP JUDGMENT

Dear friend,

Have you ever noticed how much time and energy you spend sitting in judgment of yourself and others? It's hard to take an honest look at our own judgmental patterns. We surrender so much of our time to them, yet we gain nothing positive or productive.

When I made a concentrated effort to identify just how much judgment filled my life, I was truly shocked. It seemed like criticism and comparison were practically my autopilot. The deeper I dug into my judgments, the more I uncovered that these critical thoughts stemmed from my uncertainties and insecurities. Maybe part of me felt that the judgments I held for myself wouldn't be so painful if I had them for others too. But the thing is, judgment keeps us stuck, separated, and small. Judgment wants us to believe that we aren't good enough and that we are unworthy of the good in our lives.

Can you forgive yourself today for being judgmental? And can you give yourself permission to think differently? Rather than being critical, try acceptance. Instead of negative self-talk, lean in to self-love.

Remember, **cultivate acceptance for yourself and others. Release unnecessary judgments.**

MARCH 31

THE BOSS OF YOUR LIFE

Dear friend,

I was a pretty passive child. Not overly demanding, I'd go with the flow and fly easily below the radar. I never thought anything of it until I was around eight years old. That's when my dad encouraged me to change things up; I needed to be more assertive, he said. Truthfully, I didn't take kindly to this advice! I never wanted to be forceful or forward; I was afraid of being too much.

In hindsight, I'm so grateful for that nudge from my dad. He gave me permission years ago to be confident, self-assured, and strong-willed, inviting me to become the boss of my own life.

Being the boss is a big job; it means standing up for yourself and standing up for what's right, even when it's uncomfortable. It's trusting a life path that might not make sense to others, but one that's right for you. Today, consider what would be different if you embraced being the boss of your life.

Remember, **the most important approval for you to seek is your own. Embrace this role you play in your life.**

UNCONDITIONAL SELF-LOVE

Dear friend,

Do you love yourself? I know, this is a loaded question. When I've been asked this, I've felt a variety of emotions—doubt, shame, and avoidance, to name a few.

Over the course of my life, I've been led to believe two different—both false—ideas about love. First, it's selfish and egotistical to love myself, and second, that I'm unworthy of it. So trust me when I say, I know how difficult it can be to cultivate self-love in a world that's constantly pointing out reasons not to.

Today, join me in reframing the relationship you have with yourself. First, let go of the falsehood that self-love is self-centered. Love is not a finite resource. The more we love and accept ourselves, the more love we have to give to the world.

Second, release the idea that you're not worthy of love. After many years of self-criticism and self-doubt, it's not always easy to lean in to self-love. So start small.

Can you identify one aspect of yourself that you are grateful for? It can be a characteristic, a trait, or something physical. Let that affirm your love for this part of you, knowing you are worthy of it always.

Remember, you are worthy of love in all forms. Open your heart to loving yourself fully and completely.

NOTICE RED FLAGS

Dear friend,

We hear a lot about the "red flags" that surround us—those signals or gut instincts that tell us to pay attention and check in, and sometimes to walk away. Noticing a red flag is a gift; it's useful information that can help guide choices and decisions. Red flags don't necessarily mean someone or something is bad; they might just be a warning to slow down or to regroup.

I like to think of red flags as a radar of sorts, an alert to be mindful, to get more information, and to check in to see if what's happening is actually in alignment with my desires. This may feel like a pit in my stomach after spending time with someone new or like unexplained waves of confusion or uncertainty.

As with so much in our lives, being present and connected with ourselves is how we can start to notice the red flags around us. Today, pay attention to how people, places, and situations make you feel. Does someone make you feel nervous? Are you jittery when you're in a particular place? Your intuition is wise. Cultivate and strengthen the relationship you have with yourself by honoring your gut feelings.

Remember, whispers, nudges, and hints guide you along your journey. Be open to listening to them, from moment to moment.

TRUST YOUR GREEN FLAGS

Dear friend,

We talked yesterday about red flags—signals that people, places, and circumstances aren't meant for us. Today, let's talk about "green flags"—the good omens and positive signs that let us breathe a sigh of relief, knowing that in this moment, things are okay.

When you start to notice green flags, you're learning to trust yourself, your judgment, and your gut instincts. Life is constantly showing us the good. We just have to be open, receptive, and attentive to it.

How do you do this? Pay attention to how you feel throughout your day. Notice which people make you feel good when you're in their presence. Notice the energy every time you walk into a room, and observe where you feel nurtured.

When you grow to know yourself on this deeper level, you realize what you want, what to look for, and what people and places make you feel seen, heard, and understood. Just think of your life like a laboratory: Every day, you are collecting new information. Try making it fun! It can be encouraging to welcome more of the good stuff into your life.

Remember, only *you* know what you need. Trust your instincts, your judgment, and your intuition.

LET GO OF ANTICIPATORY GRIEF

APRIL 4

Dear friend,

If you've known grief, you know it can upend your world. My entire existence changed when my dad unexpectedly passed away in his sleep. Assuming his death wouldn't come until much later in life, I was unprepared to face the reality of loss at such a young age, and I suffered immensely.

Since the passing of my dad and many other loved ones in my life, I've found myself holding on to fear and dread of what I know to be the inevitable, asking myself, *When will other people leave me too?* In short, the grief I had already experienced was pushing me into anticipatory grief for future losses.

I've found unexpected comfort when I've embraced the truth of life's impermanence rather than denying it. Knowing that life is limited, I can remember to value the people in my life in a more meaningful way. Grief has taught and prepared me to honor the presence of others right now.

Today, offer gratitude and love to the ones you love and care for. Share a simple message of appreciation for their presence—like a text message or a note—and let those you cherish know how you feel.

Remember, **embrace the moments you have with the people you love, and honor the time you have in this moment.**

YOUR WHOLENESS IS FOREVER

Dear friend,

Wherever you are on your path, you, too, are on a journey of healing. Your desire to heal may stem from traumas in your past that chipped away at your connection with your truest self, or you may want to build up who you already are. Ultimately, your life's path will bring up many feelings, questions, and uncertainties about who you are and why you are here.

Yet, despite what you may think, being on a journey of healing doesn't mean you aren't already whole or enough. Regardless of your past, and no matter what lies in your future, you are always whole and never broken. Life's circumstances may sometimes leave you feeling shattered and scattered, but know that you can never lose who you are.

Return to your truest self with deep love and compassion today, and commit to fortifying your strong foundation—your core, your values, your specific sense of *you*. Observe who you are without judgment, recognizing that you are always whole and nothing can take that away.

Remember, **nothing can diminish who you are in this world. You are always whole and worthy, no matter what.**

YOU ALREADY BELONG

APRIL 6

Dear friend,

We all yearn to find a place in this world that we belong to and that belongs to us. Yet sometimes the places where we think we should fit in easily—like our families and communities—don't quite click. Sometimes we feel that there is nowhere to go where we will be accepted as we are.

Belonging is a feeling we all crave and search for. I used to think I needed to find the right people and places that would welcome me with open arms. I thought that if I could, then I would feel at home in this world.

Certainly, whenever we find these people, it can be a wonderful gift. There is no greater feeling than genuine love and support. But if you want to experience a lasting sense of belonging, you first have to find it in yourself.

When you know and love yourself, you create the opportunity for better connections with others. You sense what is and isn't for you and build the confidence to stand up for yourself. This self-knowledge allows for better discernment in choosing your people and provides you with wisdom to pivot in and out of spaces when necessary.

Remember, **whenever you feel the pain of not belonging, take comfort in knowing that you always belong to yourself.**

REVISIT LOYALTY

Dear friend,

When we think about key virtues in healthy, successful relationships, loyalty usually rises to the top of the list. We're often told loyalty is *everything*.

Though there is value in expressing loyalty toward the people in your life who have earned it, where do you draw the line? Is it admirable to betray your own best interests in order to maintain allegiance? Can you be self-assured and confident and still be considered loyal?

These questions make me think about the concept of *blind loyalty* and what we've let it mean for our relationships: a universal endorsement of another person's behaviors, even if we don't agree with them. But let's get clear on what healthy loyalty looks like. It's being supportive of and committed to someone, but it doesn't mean condoning everything they do. You can be loyal and disagree or feel disappointed.

Today, revisit and, if you need to, reframe the position loyalty holds in your life, noticing where it has held you back or kept you from speaking your truth.

———

Remember, **the people meant to be in your life won't be scared away by your voice.**

EMBRACE IMPERFECTION

Dear friend,

    I want to let you off the hook from thinking you have to live your life perfectly. Many of us feel pressure to live a big life and do big things. In striving to live up to our potential, we hold ourselves to an unreachable standard of perfection.

    But remember, perfection is a myth. Despite our efforts to do it all and be our best, chasing perfection is a fruitless endeavor. It will run you ragged and rob you of recognizing the beauty of who you are, imperfections and all.

    So today, release yourself from seeking perfection and, instead, embrace the beautiful messiness of the present moment. In what aspects of your life can you find gratitude and love for the parts of you that might be different, knowing they make you who you are in the best way possible? How can you start to look at your life as a unique story that has meaning, purpose, and validity, no matter what?

    Perfection is overrated; lean in to your humanity and enjoy being uniquely you.

Remember, **you have nothing to prove, and you don't need to strive to be perfect. Just be you.**

PROTECT YOUR ENERGY

Dear friend,

Energy is our most precious resource in this life. We must protect it and be aware of how we are expending it. Energy is our life force, and if we overspend and deplete it, we will find ourselves burned-out, listless, and uninspired.

Here's one practice to help you protect your energy: Reevaluate your *should*s. Think of how frequently you tell yourself you should do something, big or small: *I should go to the gym today. I should call my grandmother. I should start that project.* The shoulds are endless. While harmless at their core, the shoulds pile up, covertly signaling that our efforts aren't enough. They produce guilt for not doing more or trying harder, which only begets bitterness.

When I started to eliminate the "shoulds" from my life, I felt a surge in my energy and mental clarity. I was no longer resentful and frustrated, but at peace with my ability to discern what is important and what can be let go.

If you find the shoulds are robbing you of your energy, give yourself permission to say no today. Practice protecting your peace and guarding your time.

Remember, **your energy is a precious resource; deprioritize the thoughts and activities that do not serve you.**

WHAT TO DO WITH REMORSE

APRIL 10

Dear friend,

When I started to unpack the parts of my past that had gone unexamined, I recalled some moments that brought me shame and deep remorse. I had caused harm, and it was hard for me to come to terms with that. I immediately condemned that version of myself—that was not who I wanted to be.

What do we do with these complicated feelings? Part of healing, growing, and evolving is learning to forgive ourselves for our past and releasing the temptation to carry regret and remorse into the present. We know we cannot change anything in the past, so let's stop trying.

Sometimes it's appropriate to issue an apology or reach out if it's possible. And then you can take those feelings of regret and let them fuel your wisdom moving forward. Don't let your regret stay stagnant; transform it into a lesson learned. There is no greater way to make amends and show true growth than by changing your behavior.

Let today be the day you stop criticizing yourself for the mistakes of your past and open yourself to forgiveness and acceptance. No single action defines your life's story, and it's never too late to learn, grow, and choose again.

Remember, **your power doesn't come from ruminating about what you've done wrong but from learning how to make it right.**

APRIL 11

THE IMPORTANCE OF TRUTH

Dear friend,

The importance of telling the truth is a lesson instilled in us since childhood. Still, due to self-preservation, necessity, or fear of consequences, we may feel pulled to hide the truth rather than stand in it.

Sometimes the truth is overwhelming and intimidating, so it's understandable that we would want to bend the story to keep the peace or say things we don't mean in order to maintain a certain mood. We think we're doing ourselves a service in crafting these untrue narratives, but we're often doing more harm than good. Shying away from the truth adds more stress to our lives than we realize.

Today, recall a moment when you had to remember the details of a crafted story and the anxiety that comes with it. Keeping up with all those little untruths is exhausting, right? When you embrace truthfulness, you can uncover a new sense of freedom and inner peace. You can tap into a deep well of confidence when you know your words and actions stem from reality. In so many ways, telling the truth leads to freedom.

Remember, **the truth always sets you free. Embrace it, don't hide from it.**

RELEASE THE *WHY*

Dear friend,

 I consider myself someone who likes to learn and understand. I've always been thirsty for knowledge. And while this is generally a noble trait, I'm often ruminating and seeking answers in life, and thus spending much of my energy in my head. I sometimes wear myself down searching for the *why*.

> A friend changes their tone and energy toward me. *Why?*
> Life sends me an unexpected curveball. *Why?*
> A relationship abruptly comes to a close. *Why?*

 Rather than focusing on healing and moving forward, I keep myself stuck in a loop of *why*s. Do you do this too?

 When we ask why, we may not always get the information we seek. We can't control what others share with us or what life chooses to reveal. But we do have control over the utilization of our energy. With that in mind, today, I hope you can find freedom from needing to know the why. You have the power to bring your energy back to the present moment, where you can focus on healing and moving forward.

Remember, **you can protect your peace and preserve your energy by letting go of the need to know why.**

APRIL 12

APRIL 13

BECOME A GOOD COMMUNICATOR

Dear friend,

Do you often feel misunderstood? Do you feel like people are listening but not really hearing you? It's extremely frustrating not to feel heard, and it's isolating when our communication falls flat. Clear communication connects us, while miscommunication breeds resentment.

How we communicate sets an important tone and precedent, so why do so many of us shy away from speaking from our hearts and being confident in our truths? Are we afraid of being judged? Are we afraid of being abandoned? Often, we are.

The problem is, when you don't use clear communication, your relationships suffer. But when you commit to communicating with self-awareness, presence, and clarity, while maintaining openness and vulnerability, you are presented with deeper understanding and stronger connection.

As you interact today, how can you speak more clearly and honestly? In what areas do you sense that you're holding back because of insecurity or fear? How would it feel to express yourself in *every* area of your life from a place of clarity and truth?

Remember, **the words you speak matter. Commit to speaking with confidence and conviction.**

CULTIVATE CONFIDENCE

Dear friend,

Confidence is an alluring quality. I've always been envious of those naturally confident, self-assured people, while my own self-doubt told me that self-confidence is out of reach.

Though I do think some people are born with a strong sense of it, I've realized that confidence isn't as elusive as I once thought. It's something I can build and cultivate—and you can too.

If you aren't sure how to build yourself up, consider this well-known phrase: "Fake it till you make it." How would the confident version of you enter a room, talk to people, and pursue your dreams? What energy would the confident you emit? What would an authentic, embodied, confident life look like for you?

Confidence is a practice and something we strengthen. I no longer think some of us are born with higher self-esteem; it's just that some of us make a concentrated effort to infuse confidence into our being.

Check your self-talk today. Are you cruel and critical? Do you nitpick and judge? If you're feeling a lack of confidence, your thoughts are likely reinforcing your self-doubt. Believe in yourself today.

Remember, **you have everything you need to live a self-assured life. Let your self-talk fuel your confidence.**

APRIL 15

WHEN YOU FEEL LIKE AN IMPOSTOR

Dear friend,

Why do we often feel like impostors in our own lives? We do the hard work, yet we don't feel worthy of the fruits of our labor. Why?

We've all experienced situations that have knocked us down. We've encountered people who've made us believe our inherent worth and abilities aren't real. This can lead us to think we aren't good enough—not even for the things we've already achieved and are achieving now.

This phenomenon of unnecessary doubt is called *impostor syndrome*, and today, if it is plaguing you, I hope you can gently release it. Replace your self-doubt with reminders of your worth and your efforts. Remember how much you have accomplished. Remind yourself of the skills, strengths, and qualities you already embody—a combination that is wonderfully unique to you.

I know how much work you've put into your life. I know how much you care. I know that you are worthy and good enough to be where you are.

Today, I hope you can know this too.

Remember, **you've worked so hard, and your efforts are valid. Know your worth and own your powerful place in this world.**

THE POWER OF PRACTICE

Dear friend,

You've probably heard the phrase "practice makes perfect," a common refrain we tell ourselves to maintain diligence and discipline in pursuit of our goals and dreams. We've already debunked the myth of perfectionism, so let's dig into the importance of practice. It might not lead to "perfect," but our daily rituals certainly impact who we become.

Life offers no shortcuts, and none of us is born knowing how to navigate the ups and downs of it all. To get to where we want to go, we have to work hard, put in the effort, and be willing to learn and grow through practice. Practice prepares us for what we want and moves us closer to where we want to be. It fortifies us with resiliency and gives us confidence through experience. Practice meets you where you are and takes you to a new destination, introducing you to a new version of yourself along the way.

What are you practicing daily in your life? What practices would be helpful to add to your routine? How can you honor yourself by showing up for your practices today?

Remember, **the practices you adopt have the capacity to shape who you are.**

BECOME A MAGNET FOR LOVE

Dear friend,

 I'm sure we were all exposed to fairy-tale romances from a young age, and so many of us desperately want our lives to match what we have seen on-screen. When this didn't happen for me, I took it as a sign that something was wrong with me, that maybe I wasn't lovable.

 In hindsight, I can see I was being passive in my approach to bringing people into my life. I let life happen to me, hoping someone would show up along the way. But I've since learned that I need to be an active participant. Actually, I need to be proactive and assured of my desires.

 The work I needed to do was on myself, building my confidence and self-love, fully owning who I am, and finding my place in this world. From that powerful space, I know I can be a magnet for the relationships I desire. Authenticity draws in the kind of people I always hoped for yet thought I couldn't find.

 If you're feeling frustrated or misunderstood in your relationships, know that there is always another opportunity to open yourself to new love, in all forms. Trust that your energy, your kindness, and exactly who you are will call the right people to you, at the right time.

Remember, **you are deserving of love, and it is always available to you. Be active in seeking what you desire.**

A REMINDER ABOUT ABUNDANCE

Dear friend,

Here's an odd fact about me: I rarely let myself take the last piece of anything. Last cookie in the jar? I'll leave it. One more piece of sushi on the plate? I'll always offer it to someone else. It's sad to think of all the times I held myself back from a desire because I didn't want to take up space, have more, or eat the last fry.

But the truth is, there is enough space, we are allowed to want more, and we can always order more fries if we run out.

We often think there's not enough in life to go around, that if someone else attains something we want, we can't have it. We start seeing limits to resources and feel a constant sense of lack. This scarcity mindset sets us up for disappointment, keeping us stuck and unmotivated.

Today, I want to remind you that there is enough for all of us. We all can achieve what we wish, and living with this belief will make you a magnet for what you desire. The next time you are hit with the feeling of lack, repeat to yourself, *There's more than enough to go around.*

Remember, **you are allowed to take up space, you have permission to want, and you are worthy of your desires.**

YOU WILL NOT MISS OUT

Dear friend,

    Perhaps you fear that making the wrong choice will completely knock you off your course. This all-encompassing anxiety that we can mess it all up has the capacity to leave us paralyzed with uncertainty.

    It's so common to feel that if you don't make the right choices at the right time, life will pass you by. That if you don't always say yes, you'll miss out on opportunities. That if you're not constantly going, doing, and creating, your life will feel meaningless and underwhelming.

    If you've experienced this, hold yourself with compassion. Give yourself permission to release the worry that you'll somehow miss out on your idealized life. You will never be passed over by the people, places, and experiences that are meant for you.

    Can you seek to love and honor the life you've been given? Can you trust that you will show up in your life and that life will show up for you? Be encouraged that you can trust your path, and take comfort in the flow of your own timing.

Remember, **you don't need to worry about missing out; simply show up each day with trust and confidence in your path.**

REWRITE YOUR STORY

Dear friend,

You are the main character of your own life's story. Isn't it empowering to remember this truth?

If your life were a movie, how would it be narrated? What would be the overarching themes and hurdles? Do you view yourself as a hero, a villain, or an extra? Do you see your character as someone with confidence and stature or as someone who is self-critical and filled with doubt? Do you actually want to root for yourself?

This exercise can help you become aware of the thoughts and beliefs you have about your own life. And bonus—it's fun! Use the information gathered in this imagination practice as data points for how you see yourself. Are there any unnecessary limitations you're imposing on your life's story? Are you holding yourself back with a false narrative?

If yes, then cut those storylines and rewrite the script. Never underestimate the power of your mind and the influence of your thoughts. How do you want the story of your life to unfold?

Remember, **you are the author of your story. You can always change the script.**

SAY YES TO JOY

Dear friend,

Have you ever felt like you shouldn't be allowed to feel joy? Like you don't deserve it? I once was facing deep consequences for mistakes I had made, and I couldn't quickly fix the mess. I felt overwhelmed and bogged down by the long journey of redemption ahead, mostly because I thought my mistakes precluded me from feeling joy.

Here's what I realized: Life is filled with dualities. It can be hard, and it can be happy. There can be sadness alongside contentment. There can be pain alongside pleasure. Life can be both.

The beauty of life is that you can experience it all, all at once. Today, what would change for you if you consciously invited joy into your life, even when things feel challenging and difficult? Even when you don't feel you deserve it?

As you go through the day, know that you are allowed to feel happiness regardless of hardship or your personal mistakes. You're allowed to seek silver linings and be filled with gratitude for them. You're allowed to plant seeds of happiness within yourself and let them bloom through difficulty.

Remember, **the practice of seeking joy is powerful and life-changing. The small joys of life will sustain you through hard times.**

LET GO OF JUDGMENT

Dear friend,

I know how painful and cruel life can feel. Sometimes it seems like we just can't do anything right, and we may even wonder why we try. The harshness of the world can make us feel judged, mocked, and misunderstood, all leading to an overwhelming sense of loneliness.

Out of fear of judgment or ridicule, we often dampen aspects of ourselves and anxiously seek to please in order to find acceptance. It's natural and normal to want to be liked, loved, and supported, but at what cost? When we attach our identities to the judgments of the people around us, our thoughts become consumed with worry and anguish.

It's not your life's purpose to please the world, and it's not your job to gather approval from others. You are enough, no matter what people think or say. So today, release the need to please and release the need to overthink. Focus on the ones who get you, the ones who see you for who you are and never leave you questioning your worth; they are your people.

Remember, when you release the need to worry about the opinions and judgments of others, you reclaim precious time and energy.

APRIL 23

QUIET YOUR MIND

Dear friend,

We think thousands of thoughts a day—some neutral, some repetitive and negative, and, luckily, some positive. Many of us have grown accustomed to this mental freneticism, but when our thoughts run rampant, one after another, it can become dizzying and overwhelming. (This is especially true if most of our thoughts are negative.)

When unchecked, a spiral of unproductive, repetitive thoughts can lead to burnout and overwhelm. Chronic overthinking will have you believing you have no control over the thoughts in your mind—but remember, you do.

Awareness is always the first step to change, so today, reflect on the current state of your mind. If you're exhausted, despite being well rested, it's likely that your mind is working overtime. If you're struggling to make decisions or are distracted easily, your mind probably needs a break.

While you can't completely quiet your mind, you can start to choose what does and does not take space in your brain. If your thoughts are running away from you, remember your power of choice, from moment to moment. What thought pattern can you choose right now so you can arrive at peace?

Remember, **you don't have to live at the mercy of an overactive mind. Give your brain a break and find peace in the pause.**

YOUR FEELINGS ARE VALID

Dear friend,

Our feelings can often seem elusive or confusing. We often ask ourselves, *What's making me feel this way? Why am I experiencing this emotion?*

Sometimes we know exactly why we feel a certain way, and we can identify the particular situations that produced our feelings. When sad or tragic things happen, we know we will feel somber. When happy moments arise, we expect celebratory emotions.

And then feelings surface, and we don't know why or where they came from. We can be completely at peace when, suddenly, a wave of sadness or overwhelm washes over us without warning. We can be triggered out of the blue and experience a mood change instantly.

Try not to judge yourself for the emotions you are feeling; they are valid even if you can't explain them. Experiencing a full array of emotions is core to the human experience. Today, as you manage your feelings, welcome what they have to say to you.

Remember, **you don't have to apologize for how you feel; you are responsible only for how you act on those feelings.**

PRIORITIZE RESPECT

Dear friend,

I used to think meaningful relationships stemmed from likability and common values. Or simply how much fun we had. But over time I've come to understand that those external qualities aren't always manageable and don't always signify compatibility.

Now, whenever I think about what I desire most and how I ultimately want to feel in my interactions, I believe the most important component of a meaningful relationship is mutual respect.

Cultivating respect for ourselves and other people feels like a wiser and more sustainable way of creating meaningful connections. With respect at the center of any relationship, we can hold space for one another even with the possibility of disagreement. Through respect, we can honor each other's lived experiences—however different they may be—and appreciate the complexities of human emotion.

Ask yourself what respect looks like for you in your daily life. How can you respectfully create space for others so you can coexist in this life? How can you live so that others feel called to be respectful of you? We all deserve to live harmoniously through our differences. Notice how it feels to give and receive respect.

Remember, **mutual respect will blossom in your relationships when you start from a place of self-respect.**

YOUR BODY IS YOUR HOME

APRIL 26

Dear friend,

What a beautiful life we live, where each one of us inhabits a unique body, created just for us, just for this life. Yet how maddening to live in a world that teaches us to critique our bodies, pinpoint our faults, and criticize our features, and that makes us feel like the skin we live in is never enough.

I've spent much of my life at war with my body, wishing it could be different somehow and very rarely acknowledging the miracle that it actually is.

The truth is, your body is your home, the encasing of your soul, and your mode of transport through this life. Your body is a gift and should be treated as such.

We all feel the pressure to change our bodies somehow. We tend to believe we *could* love our bodies, if only something about it were different. But what would your life look like if you embraced your body, your home, exactly as it is in this moment? Can you imagine a life where you treated your body like the miracle that it is?

Remember, **you deserve love exactly as you are and to feel at home within yourself.**

APRIL 27

UNDERSTAND YOUR IMPACT

Dear friend,

Picture this: Someone walks into a room and completely changes the mood. They approach you and make a passing comment, and your inner state flips upside down. Has this happened to you? Or have you done this to someone else?

As someone who is easily influenced by other people's moods and energies, I have become keenly aware of how my energy impacts other people. I am known to be a bit moody—I am a Scorpio, after all—so I try to be aware of my energy change in a situation and notice how it impacts other people.

While I believe we have the power to decide how we show up in life, it's natural to be influenced by moods—our own and others'. The trick to navigating this is becoming aware of others' influence on us—for better and for worse. This way, we can make a choice about how to respond.

Likewise, be intentional about the kind of energy you put into a room. Know your power and honor it, being mindful of how you influence and impact others. Take responsibility for showing kindness and respect, and observe whether others follow your cue. This will help create the healthy relationships you crave and a more peaceful existence.

Remember, **your energy is powerful, and you have an impact. Be responsible for what you put into the world.**

DON'T BE A VICTIM

Dear friend,

People can be cruel; that's an unfortunate truth of life. Disappointment, betrayal, and deceit are devastating to experience. I know I'm not alone in facing these deep hurts.

When I was a child, my mom and I had many conversations about the unfair nature of life and overcoming unjust situations. She said something to me that has forever been burned into my mind. She told me that, yes, I can be and have been victimized by the actions of other people, but those actions do not have to shape who I am.

"Don't let yourself be a victim," she said.

I had to absorb this lesson because, in reality, I had been victimized. This differentiation helped me not to allow my trauma to define me but rather to empower me. I came to understand that I never wanted to let what happens to me have a say in who I am. This realization has allowed me to change my viewpoint altogether.

No matter what life has presented to you or where you are on your healing journey, know that the hurtful actions of others never get to decide who you are. Find empowerment and strength in knowing that no one has that power but you.

Remember, there are so many beautiful moments in your life's story. *You* get to decide which moments will define you.

HEALING FROM HEARTACHE

Dear friend,

After one particular breakup years ago, I thought I would spend the rest of my life feeling sad. I believed my mind would never let go of the heartbreak. I simply thought it was my lot in life to live with this type of pain.

But just like with all fleeting emotions, those feelings of heartache passed with time. My wounds healed, and new memories and opportunities presented themselves.

If you are going through heartache or holding on to something from the past that won't let you go, know that so many people in this world are waiting to love and know you. Whatever hurt you've experienced will one day heal, your heart will mend, and you will experience the love, kindness, and support that you deserve and yearn for.

Broken relationships often make us feel unworthy or unlovable. I want you to know this isn't true. You are always worthy. It's just that not all relationships are meant to last.

Remember, **heartbreak doesn't have to break you; it can crack you open and help you to begin again.**

MANAGING TIME

Dear friend,

Do you ever feel like time is rushing past you? Days turn to weeks turn to years, and before we know it, it feels like life has passed us by. While it's true that we cannot control time, we can manage our relationship with it. That feels powerful, doesn't it?

As we know, we can't change what we're not aware of. So ask yourself, *What relationship do I have with time? Do I feel like time is a limited resource, or does it feel abundant and plentiful? Am I always racing the clock, or do I feel peaceful and on time?* Be honest and clear with your answers, because this is how you can start to make changes where needed.

Feeling like you just don't have enough time is a signifier that something is amiss. What is happening in your life, right now, that you feel you can't accomplish or that won't happen for you? How can you start to be intentional with your time so that you never feel like it's being wasted?

Remember, **you don't have to resist the concept of time. Trust how life is unfolding.**

MAY 1

SELF-CARE IS NOT SELFISH

Dear friend,

Many of us struggle with the seemingly simple notion of self-care. I often wonder why. We all deserve true, meaningful nourishment—nurturing habits, practices of mindfulness, and feel-good routines that nurture our souls. So how is it possible that we wouldn't act in self-love and self-care?

In my contemplation, I realized that many of us were never taught the value of self-care. In fact, I think we're often told the opposite—that focusing on ourselves isn't important. Some would even call it selfish.

Today, we change the narrative. Contrary to what you were made to believe, it is not selfish or egotistical to love yourself. Release the notion that taking time for yourself will take away from the love, kindness, and care you wish to extend to others. In truth, learning to love yourself will help you to better love others.

Can you release any guilt or shame you hold for desiring self-love? You're allowed to be a priority in your life; you're allowed to honor your needs.

Remember, **the more you care for yourself, the more you can show up for your life and the people in it.**

GO WITH THE FLOW

Dear friend,

I've been on a mission lately to follow the path of least resistance and lean in to a calmer flow in my life. I want to experience more of the freeing feeling that comes when I stop resisting *what is* and learn to accept the experiences that come my way.

As we know, we must take action to get the things we want, but I think, as human beings, we tend to glorify the struggle and the grind. We place so much value in hustle and productivity. We believe good things can't be easy and, subsequently, inflict unnecessary suffering on ourselves.

I invite you to join me on this mission to go with the flow. What could this look like? Leaning back when you feel the knee-jerk urge to micromanage or control. Breathing through frustration rather than lashing out. Holding on to trust and optimism for your life path instead of doubt and uncertainty.

As you work on being present in the now, you will see signs, synchronicities, and opportunities in front of you. With renewed presence, you can breathe a sigh of relief, knowing you are always at the right place at the right time. Today, be open to guidance.

Remember, **even though life is difficult, we can still approach it with ease and flow.**

LET YOUR ANGER FUEL YOU

Dear friend,

    I used to be afraid of my anger. When it would arise in difficult situations, I thought it was bad and wrong to feel this way, so I would push it aside and bury it with pleasantness and false notions of positivity.

    Just like with all feelings, anger has a powerful role in our lives, if we pay attention to it. Our feelings are data points, indicating to us what matters most, what changes we'd like to make, and how we wish to show up in the world.

    Rather than avoiding anger and ignoring that data, collect it like you would if you were a scientist. Take note when something bothers you. Consider what's happening or what you want to happen when you feel anger arise. There is always something to learn when we approach life with curiosity.

    As you go about your day today, pay attention to your feelings. What could they be telling you about your priorities, your dreams, and what your heart is longing to see in the world?

Remember, **all feelings give you information about yourself. Welcome even the difficult ones.**

TRUST YOUR TIMING

Dear friend,

It hasn't been easy for me to fully lean in and accept all the circumstances of my life. As I've shared, I resisted, questioned, and judged so much of my reality. So when I say this to you, know that it has taken me a long time to get here, and it has required a lot of inner work and practice.

I wholeheartedly trust the timing of my life.

It's shocking to me that I can say that. I lived a long time thinking I was forgotten or left behind. But day by day, step by step, I built up a strong belief in myself and my path, and it's been one of my most rewarding ventures yet.

How can you start to trust the timing of your life, especially when you've been accustomed to comparing or judging it? Begin with gratitude for what is good *now*, and think of all you've been through and accomplished. Reinforce patience and presence in your daily life, knowing you are always making progress. Lastly, seek to love the path that's been given to you, fully and completely. How does that feel?

Remember, **the timing of your life won't fail you; what is for you will never miss you.**

THE POWER OF SELF-FORGIVENESS

Dear friend,

When you think of forgiveness, what comes to mind? Maybe you imagine it as a response or closure to painful situations. You likely know how beneficial it is to yourself and your relationships to heal the wounds of the past. But how often do you think about forgiving yourself?

We often are our own harshest critics, holding ourselves to unrealistic standards, rehashing our shortcomings over and over again. Do we ever stop to give ourselves grace? Mistakes are inevitable. It's going to be painful, embarrassing, and agonizing. Even so, remember that these errors in judgment are a necessary part of life. Going the wrong way shows us how good life can feel when we choose the right way.

Holding on to regret won't change the past. It will just unnecessarily carry your pain into your present and future. When you forgive yourself, you create space to choose better, to be better, to use the knowledge you've gained for good, and to empower yourself to be more in control of your actions.

What do you need to forgive yourself for today?

Remember, **you deserve to be set free from your past so you can live a better present.**

LEAN IN TO LEARNING

Dear friend,

Isn't it funny that, as kids, we were sent to school to learn and gain wisdom, but we did so grudgingly? Learning often felt like a chore and sometimes a bore. But now, as an adult, I find myself constantly seeking new information. I yearn for the days filled with learning and absorbing knowledge!

Still, rather than looking back on my school years with regret, I've decided that a better way to spend my time is by considering myself a lifelong learner, and I hope I can continue to be a student of life, regardless of my age.

Isn't it amazing that there is always something new to learn? The world is filled with endless information. How often do we find ourselves embracing all there is to offer? Ask yourself where you'd like to be a student. What piques your interest and excites your curiosity? Let yourself lean in to learning, and let it open your mind to new worlds and new outlooks.

Remember, gaining wisdom, at any age, is priceless. You are never too old to learn something new.

WHEN TO LET PEOPLE IN

Dear friend,

Have you ever outgrown a friendship or another type of relationship? As we build a deep, loving relationship with ourselves, we also develop a keen discernment of who to let into our lives and who might have overstayed their welcome.

Our desires for love, connection, and community might lead us to be more flexible with our standards and boundaries than we should. It's common to seek quantity over quality when it comes to friends. But know you deserve to have and uphold standards for the people who are close to you.

Of course, we go through trial and error with people and have our hearts broken. But never let the relationships that soured make you believe there aren't people out there waiting to cheer you on.

The people who are meant for you will respect you and honor you, follow through on their commitments to you, understand your boundaries and personal limits, be trustworthy, and allow you to grow and evolve with them. Today, look for and appreciate the people who light you up with their presence and make you remember your worth.

Remember, **you are not alone in this world; each day is a chance to bring someone new into your life who will love you in infinite ways.**

IT'S OKAY NOT TO BE OKAY

Dear friend,

Is today an up-day or a down-day? Life is full of highs and lows, of good and bad, and we can't predict what the future holds. If you're not feeling on top of the world today, let yourself off the hook and cut yourself some slack.

Many of us hold ourselves to a standard of perpetually appearing cool, calm, and collected. We want to seem like we have it all together, and we can feel shame when we struggle. Some of us were taught to push aside our feelings and were made to believe that our sensitivity was a weakness. But being human is complicated and will bring up complex emotions.

I want you to know that it's okay not to be okay sometimes. I want you to know that your work and your efforts are enough, and just because some days feel challenging, it doesn't mean you're doing anything wrong. Don't let anyone tell you that you must have it all together, all the time. Treat yourself with care and understanding, and take comfort that however you're feeling today, it's okay.

Remember, **you are a human being with complicated emotions; don't let them define you or make you think you're not enough.**

BE PURPOSEFUL WITH YOUR TIME

Dear friend,

If there's one thing we know for certain, it's that our time on Earth is finite. We are here for only a little while, so let's make the most of it!

One of the most powerful ways you can honor the precious resource of time is by becoming more discerning toward what you do with it. It's empowering to know that you can decide where you'll spend your energy.

If you say yes to everything and everyone, blindly giving away your time and energy, you may find yourself drained and bitter in the process. Not every request is worthy of your time. You can feel confident to discern what matters most and let the rest go.

The trick to discernment is noticing how you feel from moment to moment. Take inventory of which situations and circumstances make you feel purposeful, and use that information to influence your choices.

Today, ask yourself, *Are there places in my life where I say yes when I want to say no?*

Remember, **you can't control the passing of time, but you do have the power to choose how you spend it.**

ACCEPT SUPPORT

Dear friend,

Sometimes we feel the need to be hyper-independent, taking on monumental challenges to prove our abilities and worth. We convince ourselves that going solo is the best way to confirm our value. But the fleeting sense of pride we experience from these accomplishments is often quickly overshadowed by the inevitable cloud of burnout.

Does this experience resonate with you? It's exhausting, isn't it? (Not to mention lonely!) Remember, it's more than okay to ask for support. Find peace in knowing that you don't have anything to prove in this world and that you're not going to win the competition of life by doing everything on your own.

So many people want to cheer you on, help you out, and give you the support you deserve. You may even find that you prefer sharing your accomplishments with others. Bottom line, you aren't meant to always be alone, and as human beings, we need one another. Today, open yourself to receiving the gift of help.

Remember, **allow others to support you on your journey. You deserve aligned relationships that make you feel less alone in this world.**

THE FREEDOM OF DETACHMENT

Dear friend,

Have you ever felt that someone was desperate to get what they wanted from you? Maybe it was an acquaintance who was pushy to get a coffee date on the books, or a coworker requesting time to pick your brain, even though you mentioned your busy schedule. How did it make you feel when someone wouldn't take no for an answer?

Now, as uncomfortable as this might feel, think about times when you've been this way: attached to specific outcomes, scrambling to make a situation work, white-knuckling your desires into existence. Recalling my own moments of hyper-attachment gives me a pit in my stomach.

There's a fine line between determination and desperation—a point where passion tips into obsession. Notice where you might be holding too tightly to specific outcomes, and try to dig into the feelings underneath that: Is it fear? Confusion? Lack of trust? Remind yourself that these feelings are natural, but the attachments won't get you closer to your desires.

Seek to show up to your life with confidence and trust, knowing you're worthy of your desires and you'll never have to force what's right for you.

Remember, **you can love, care, and show up for life without unhealthy attachment.**

RECOGNIZE SELF-SABOTAGE

Dear friend,

Sometimes we pick up certain practices and coping mechanisms to get through seasons of life, and once those seasons come to a close, they are no longer needed. It's natural to hold on to old ways of living, but they can keep us from the things we really want in life. They become a means of self-sabotage and can prevent our happiness and evolution.

So how can you know which practices to keep and which to release?

Take note of your repeated tasks and routines and notice how they make you feel. Do the items on your list help you live your life to the fullest, or do they bring your spirits down? Are they pushing you toward who you want to be?

You are constantly evolving into who you are meant to be, and some habits and behaviors that once served the past versions of you may not work anymore. It's okay to let them go. Your ability to discern what is and isn't for you, especially as your life evolves, will allow you to create space for all the good to come.

Remember, each chapter of your life has purpose and meaning. Grab on to the lessons of the past and be open to a new future.

HONOR YOUR UNIQUE PATH

Dear friend,

It feels like we are given a formula for life: Go to school, get a degree, fall in love, buy a home, have children, retire. This playbook often presents itself as the only way to live a successful, meaningful life. The pressure to live up to this prescribed path is stressful and overwhelming.

What happens when your life deviates from societal norms? What happens when you don't even *want* your life to fall into that timeline?

Truthfully, my life path hasn't unfolded as I expected it to. I've often felt left behind and overlooked, but I've found so much comfort in trusting my own journey and believing my life won't betray me.

Today, take heart in knowing that your path doesn't have to look like anyone else's. You get to choose your own adventure, and you get to decide how you want your life to look and feel. Isn't that exciting? Your path isn't paved like everyone else's, and your journey will take you places that might not line up with other people's standards.

But that doesn't matter, so long as they live up to your own.

Remember, **your life is unique and messy and magical and yours.**

ENTITLEMENT VERSUS CONFIDENCE

Dear friend,

In the world we live in, it can often feel like people are overly selfish, entitled, and demanding. It's easy to criticize this behavior, and it's even worse when we realize we might be part of the problem. I hear from so many people who are exasperated by this energy: *How did we get here? Why are we like this?*

I believe the root of entitlement is unmet desire—which isn't necessarily a bad thing! It's what we do with these unmet desires that matters most. Do we push others down and out to get what we want? Or do we pursue our wants with a spirit of hard work and respect? Entitlement says, "My needs matter." But confidence says, "My needs are important, and yours are too."

In short, entitlement is the pursuit of our desires at the expense of others; confidence is the pursuit of our desires to the collective benefit of all. This differentiation has allowed me to remember the importance of true confidence, not entitlement.

How can you show up in pursuit of what you want and simultaneously make space for the wants and needs of others?

Remember, **we are all worthy of our wishes and desires. There is room for us all to succeed.**

LET LIFE BE UNCERTAIN

Dear friend,

Did you always know what you wanted to be when you grew up? I've found my own life to be a little mysterious. I never had that one dream job or deep desire that lit my path and guided me. I didn't necessarily know what I wanted to do or where I wanted to be, and for the longest time, I thought this was abnormal. People around me seemed to feel so certain and confident in their life path, and I was envious that they really *knew*. I felt ashamed of my uncertainty, like I didn't have it together.

As life progressed, I opened myself to the blessing and flexibility of uncertainty, believing that my life is no less worthy when the path is unclear. I started to embrace that the journey to clarity is just as valuable as the clarity itself.

If your life feels murky or uncertain, can you find value in the unknown? Can you find excitement for what could be rather than fearing what you don't know?

Remember, **your life isn't planned out, and you don't have to know all the answers. Let life surprise you; be open to good things beyond your imagination.**

MANAGING DISRESPECT

MAY 16

Dear friend,

How do you react to disrespect? For me, it really ruffles my feathers when I feel slighted. Many of us believe mutual respect, kindness, and compassion are the cornerstones of building meaningful, productive relationships, but not everyone feels the same.

If you're grappling with disrespect in your relationships, know that you're not alone, and the key to fostering healthier interactions is understanding how to address and overcome these toxic dynamics.

First, if you've ever felt disrespected, you should know it is not your fault; you never deserve to be treated with anything other than kindness and care. When faced with disrespect from someone else, try to remember that how other people treat you is not a reflection of your value or worth. People's actions signify who *they* are, not who you are.

Second, know that you are not responsible for how other people act, but you are responsible for how you respond. Defuse disrespect by taking space, speaking your truth, and setting clear boundaries.

Remember, **you don't have to tolerate disrespect in your relationships. Give yourself permission to stand up for yourself when your values are in question.**

MEET PEOPLE WHERE THEY ARE

Dear friend,

I'm truly fascinated that we all can exist at the same time yet view the world so differently. Our perceptions are unique to us all, but admittedly, it's confusing when we can't see eye to eye with the people around us. Deep pain and frustration arise when people we love don't see life the way we do.

Conflict and disagreement are nothing new; we know they are part of the human experience. It does feel, however, like there is less space in our world for differences, often creating unmendable holes in our relationships.

What has helped me manage this complicated dynamic is knowing that each of us has our own set of views based on our unique set of experiences. Rather than trying to change people, can we pursue acceptance?

Seeking to meet people where they are is a bridge to understanding and compassion. Today, can you seek to approach life with an open mind and an open heart? How can the energy of your relationships change with this simple shift?

Remember, we are all on different paths, learning and evolving at our own pace. Embody grace for yourself and others.

WHAT IS JEALOUSY TELLING YOU?

Dear friend,

When I was a teenager, I felt one of the worst qualities you could have was jealousy. Everyone seemed to look down on the person who always acted from a jealous place. Since that time so many years ago, I've pushed away any creeping notions of jealousy, for fear of what it might signify in me.

As an adult, with a fully formed brain, I can rationalize and realize the importance of all feelings and emotions, jealousy included. I truly believe that every feeling that surfaces within us is trying to tell us something. But are we listening?

I spent years ignoring what jealousy was telling me. I didn't realize that jealousy in itself isn't bad; what matters is how I act on it. Jealousy signals to us, at least from my experience, an untapped desire.

Do you find yourself feeling jealous of someone? Release the judgment for feeling this way, and dive a little deeper into what it is about that person that triggered your jealousy. Is it how they relate to others? Is it their external success? Take this information as a clue to help focus your life. This is using your jealousy for good.

Remember, **all feelings, even the difficult ones, have purpose in your life. Let yourself feel without avoidance or judgment.**

THE WORDS YOU SPEAK

Dear friend,

Sometimes we forget how powerful we are, how much we matter, and how much we impact the people around us. Today, remember that everything you do has importance; what you put into the world has meaning. You make waves being who you are.

This is why it's so important to remember the power of your words.

Everything in life has energy, our words included. The words we speak and write have an impact. Our words influence our future thoughts and actions. They have a ripple effect on our lives and the lives of others.

When speaking to people, and even to yourself, be mindful of what you say and how you say it. Notice how you feel and the energy you emit through your words, and ask yourself if your words align with who you are and what you want.

Today, turn to these questions from Mary Ann Pietzker's *Miscellaneous Poems*[1] as a guide to mindfully choosing your words:

> Is it true?
> Is it kind?
> Is it necessary?

Remember, you have the power to create seismic shifts and change through your words.

THE POWER IN YOUR CHOICES

MAY 20

Dear friend,

You make thousands of choices every day. You choose where to place your energy, who to be around, where to spend your money, and how to show up in the world. Your choices are your power. The thoughts you think, the actions you take, and the moves you make are meaningful.

Knowing this to be true, ask yourself, *Am I making choices and expending my energy in a way that aligns with my values, desires, and needs?*

Notice the answers that come up and consider small changes you can make to align more closely to who you are and who you want to be. Maybe this means carving out time to journal for clarity or exploring a long-desired hobby, or it could look like taking something off the table that's been adding stress to your life.

While the big decisions you make certainly matter, the small, everyday steps you take often have greater impact. Find empowerment today in knowing that the choices you make in this moment are getting you closer to all that you desire.

Remember, **every choice you make has power. You are moving toward your values, desires, and goals.**

IT'S OKAY TO BE WRONG

Dear friend,

I recently conducted an interview and stated something factually inaccurate. I was corrected in the moment and was absolutely mortified. Despite the fact that the mistake itself was no big deal, I was filled with embarrassment. A part of me wants to be right, all the time. Perhaps it's my inner people-pleaser, or maybe it's an attempt to find control in the uncontrollable. Can you relate?

Since that interview, I've done a deep dive into what it is that brings me so much shame when I make an honest mistake. Somehow I've let being wrong equate to being bad, unqualified, an impostor, and not enough. If this sounds familiar, I want you to know that this is not true. In fact, it's okay to be wrong.

Being wrong is not only unavoidable; it's also an opportunity to gain wisdom and humility. We will all be wrong at some point, and that's great! Mistakes provide space for growth and expansion, if we are open to it. A sense of collaboration comes when we are receptive to being taught and being corrected.

If you find yourself being wrong about something today, how can you be open to receiving the gifts of correction, collaboration, and growth?

Remember, it's okay for you to be wrong. Your mistakes are opportunities for you to grow and learn.

SPEND TIME WITH YOURSELF

MAY 22

Dear friend,

    I used to believe being alone meant I wasn't wanted by other people—almost like perpetual rejection. I was often embarrassed by an empty calendar and would feel anxiety about alone time, considering it a bad thing. I hadn't yet realized that blessings come from being in my own company and from honoring myself in my solitude.

    When I am alone, I connect to myself and understand who I am in a deeper way. I am reminded of my worthiness. I restore my energy and find gratitude for the little things in life. There is great purpose in being alone, because it helps me strengthen the relationship that matters most—the one I have with myself.

    What could you gain from spending some time alone today? How can you reframe your alone time to be something that nurtures and strengthens you instead of something that embarrasses you or brings you down? Imagine the possibilities that will unravel for you as you come to value your own company.

Remember, **you have much to offer this world. Enjoy the privilege of spending time with yourself and getting to know exactly who you are.**

BE GRATEFUL

Dear friend,

A few years ago, I was in a dark, depressed place. It wasn't because of some big, terrible event. In fact, from the outside it looked like things were going well. But inside I felt sad and listless, and no matter how hard I tried, I couldn't shake it.

During this time, with therapy and professional support, I actively committed to practicing gratitude. I recognized that my brain was working against me, making me believe I had nothing to be grateful for. So to fight back, I doubled down on my appreciation.

I sought out a thankful spirit in all areas of my life. I was grateful for my morning coffee. I smiled at the birds that chirped outside my window. I felt relief and joy from the purring of my geriatric cat. While giving thanks didn't magically solve my problems, it did keep me afloat—like a life raft in deep waters.

This is the power of gratitude.

I won't claim that there is a cure-all for all our sticky mental health challenges. Still, gratitude can be an amazing tool. When life feels like it's too much and gratitude feels impossible, maybe it's time to double down and seek the tiny joys of life.

Remember, there's always something to be grateful for; you just have to look for it.

NEW PERSPECTIVE, NEW LIFE

MAY 24

Dear friend,

I find it fascinating how unique each of us is. Though we all share certain experiences and milestones, I love just how differently we each view life and interpret the world around us. Yet sometimes we get so caught up in our own stories and viewpoints that we block ourselves from new perspectives. It's easy to fall into tunnel vision—so focused on our own lives that we forget to look upward and outward for inspiration and advice.

Whenever I get stuck in this way, I try to change my perspective and view the circumstances from a different angle. This can look like reexamining the facts from a new personal lens, reaching out to a trusted loved one who can offer a different viewpoint, or even moving my body physically to change my surroundings, prompting a creative flow.

The answers we seek are often right in front of us, but sometimes we need an openness to new vantage points to uncover them. Today, consider viewing life through a different lens, and notice the possibilities and opportunities that come from changing your perspective.

Remember, **there are infinite ways to live this life. Be open to a new view and a new way of living.**

WEATHERING LIFE'S STORMS

Dear friend,

Human existence is filled with dualities. We cannot have happiness without sadness or highs without lows or pleasure without pain. As much as we wish otherwise, life is not a series of happy, even-keeled events. We have sunny moments but also stormy days, and it's impossible to predict which will come next.

So how do we manage?

It's easy to feel like we are victims of our hardships. *What did I do to deserve this?* But rather than battling life's storms, can you seek to accept the rain instead? Not in a passive way but in a grounded, confident manner that says you know difficulty is a natural part of life; it isn't personal.

This is true inner strength. Approaching turbulent times from this perspective will offer you unwavering peace. The storms you are weathering today will end. The sun will shine through the clouds, and you'll bask in the light once again. This, too, will pass.

Remember, **no storm lasts forever. You are strong enough to weather your life, and your rainbow will soon come.**

IT'S YOUR LIFE

Dear friend,

When I was about five years old, my stepfather once attempted to (in my opinion) unfairly discipline me. We had a contentious relationship, and in that moment, I remember defiantly replying, "You're not the boss of me." Shocked with my response, he looked to my mom, who had a smile of agreement with me. She had taught me to stand up for myself and not be pushed around. No one had the power to name who I was.

There have been many times since when I didn't have such confidence. But the seed was planted in me long ago, and today, I hope to grow it within you: You are responsible for your own life. Of course, there are rules, guidelines, and responsibilities to abide by in order to live harmoniously with others. But following these rules doesn't mean ceding your power to do what you believe is right. You get to live for yourself; you don't have to dim who you are to please others.

Connect with yourself and explore the areas where you might be living for someone else at the expense of your own well-being. Tap into your dreams and ideals, and remember that you're allowed to follow the yearnings of your soul.

Remember, your life is yours and yours alone. You have the power to choose your adventure and course correct at any time.

THE FEARLESS VERSION OF YOU

Dear friend,

Who do you think of when you hear the word *fearless*? It's easy to idealize historical heroes for their bravery and strength, forgetting that these humans, too, had fears. What made them appear fearless was the fact that they kept going anyway, even when they were scared.

Believe it or not, there's a fearless version of you. So I ask you, What would your life look like if you didn't let fear boss you around? Who would you be if you didn't allow fear to be in the driver's seat? Where would you go if you knew the doors of life were always open to you? As you respond, notice the answers that come to mind when asking yourself these questions. Every time I answer these for myself, I'm surprised by what I learn when I release my fear.

Take your answers and let them fuel you to push through whatever might be holding you back. Let your answers guide you toward everything you desire. You're allowed to be the person you want to be and live the life that's true for you, and you're allowed to start today.

Remember, **life is short, and tomorrow is never promised. If there is something you desire, you can take action on it today.**

PLUG IN TO YOU

Dear friend,

In our highly technological world, we use our devices every day, and at night we plug them in to charge their batteries. We know how important it is to have a full battery, and we all have had those dreadful moments of accidentally forgetting to charge overnight.

Keeping this in mind, ask yourself how often you think about charging your own battery, day in and day out. Of course, you are not a device with a physical battery, but you do have finite resources. Your energy, time, and well-being are not limitless; you must be mindful of how you spend your resources and be proactive in your own self-care.

The next time you plug in one of your devices, allow it to serve as a reminder that you, too, deserve time to connect and recharge. You spend so much time giving, doing, and living on the go, but notice how good it feels to receive, stop, and be in your own presence. How does it feel to honor yourself with real self-care?

Take note of what happens when you start to prioritize your energy, and be sure to recharge as often as you need it.

Remember, **you're allowed to take time for yourself. Unplug from the external world and plug in to you.**

MAY 28

BEAUTY IN THE BREAKDOWN

Dear friend,

When I first ventured into the world of personal development, I thought it would be a small chapter in the story of my life. I believed that healing was one and done, something to tick off a list. That if I did enough work on myself, I could go through life in endless ease and peace. I quickly learned, however, that this is simply not the case. Self-development is a lifelong mission—something we are always working on and moving through rather than a small task on our to-do lists.

But there is beauty in the journey of our development—in the highs and the lows, in the breakthroughs and the breakdowns. If we didn't have the ugly and unpleasant moments in life, how could we truly appreciate those beautiful, euphoric ones? The breakdowns provide a meaningful contrast, showing us where our work still lies and, ultimately, where we have room to grow.

I believe we are never finished learning and growing, and our growth is not always linear. Whether we like it or not, new opportunities for healing are always possible. Allow yourself grace and kindness, trusting you are always being guided.

Remember, breakdowns teach you valuable lessons about your life and serve as reminders that you don't have to be perfect.

IT'S OKAY NOT TO BE LIKED

Dear friend,

If you're like me and typically can't stand it when someone doesn't like you, I'll let you in on something: It's actually okay not to be liked by everyone. Breathe that in.

I hope you felt even a small sense of relief in reading that sentence. Your worth and your ability to be loved will never depend on someone else's opinion of you. You don't have to spend your time seeking acceptance and approval from others.

When relationships in my life ended, I agonized about the *why*, taking it all personally. I nitpicked every aspect of my life, trying to determine the unlikable quality that might have pushed that person away. I was consumed with seeking out answers. Ultimately, I made these perceived rejections so much more painful than they needed to be, because the simple fact of life is, everything changes and relationships end.

Today, pursue the inner freedom of understanding that not everyone will like you, and sometimes, that won't have anything to do with you. And even if it does, it is okay. You don't need to seek universal approval or acceptance, so long as you love and accept yourself.

Remember, it's not your job to make people like you. It's your job to do everything you can to like, honor, and accept yourself.

DREAMS COME TRUE

Dear friend,

Do you remember how you felt as a child, unencumbered by the stresses and responsibilities of life? What did you desire back when you didn't put limits on yourself? Can you remember the excitement you felt when you truly believed anything was possible?

As we grow older, we often let go of those childlike dreams and ideals in pursuit of a life that is expected of us. It's easy to develop a mindset that what we truly want is out of reach or simply not possible. Things don't always turn out the way we once hoped, and we start to believe our deepest desires are foolish.

But how would your life change if you realized that's just not true? And if you allowed yourself to honor those childlike wishes and aspirations?

Imagine today that your childhood dreams have all come true. How do you feel? Is it excitement? Creativity? Bravery? Embrace this feeling and start to claim it as your own, right now. You can be a match—sparking your desires into existence—when you act and feel as if they've already happened. And really, isn't life more fun that way?

Remember, **you choose your dreams, and you can start living as if your dreams are already a reality. The rest will follow suit.**

RELEASE EXPECTATIONS

Dear friend,

You are important to this world, and you bring so much value just by being you.

This is true for all of us, so why do we frequently feel pressure to please others and live our lives the way other people want us to live?

It's hard enough to navigate the complexities of our existence, but they are made even more difficult when we spend our one beautiful life trying to satisfy the unspoken standards of someone else.

If you're stuck in the anxiety, exhaustion, and confusion that come from trying to please everyone else in your life, take in the truth of these words today:

> You don't need to live up to other people's expectations.
> You don't need to make everyone around you happy.
> You don't need to be the person other people want you to be.
> Your own needs are valid and important.
> You can say no, slow down, and prioritize your desires.

So breathe, and set the intention to simply be yourself today, fully and unapologetically.

Remember, you deserve to be known for exactly who you are. Don't mold or change yourself for anyone.

PERMISSION TO BE UNAVAILABLE

Dear friend,

As technology evolves and life changes, so do the expectations and demands put on us. We are able to connect with one another at all times, from all places, for any reason.

In theory, this is a gift. The blessings of human connection are infinite. But it also creates a new necessity for boundaries and personal limits. Technology, social media, and limitless connection with the external world can push us to be "on" 24/7. In the past, we would clock out, shut down, or unplug, but we now live in a time when we are always reachable.

Just because these advances have provided you with the opportunity to be reached at all times doesn't mean you need to make yourself available. Remember that you are allowed to set limits in every aspect of your life, including how much you engage, interact, and show up. You are in control of your time. Protecting your energy and conserving your peace require being mindful of who has access to you and when.

Remember, **you're allowed to set boundaries, unplug, and take time for you. Protect your peace.**

NOTICE YOUR CRAVINGS

Dear friend,

What are you craving? I know we commonly think of cravings in relation to food. (Maybe you've just started to think about what you'll have for lunch.) But diving a little deeper, ask yourself what your soul is craving, from the inside out. What parts of your life need a little extra nourishment?

It's easy to fall into an autopilot mindset, so it's important to be proactive in attending to our needs. Healthy routines and habits serve us well; they keep us on track and ensure we are staying true to our goals. But don't let the routine of life cut you off from the cravings that arise during your journey.

Carve out a moment for silence and stillness today, listening for the yearnings of your soul. Maybe you're craving rest or excitement or calm; you won't know until you take some intentional time to be still with yourself. In slowing down and taking a pause, you create space for unexpected wants. Let yourself honor those cravings, acting on them and giving yourself permission to pursue them.

Remember, **you are ever-changing, and your wants, desires, and needs are fluid. Honor who you are and what you want in each moment.**

WHEN YOU'RE TRIGGERED

Dear friend,

With all the situations we face daily, we're bound to run into a person or circumstance that triggers us emotionally. We all have unique pain points stored within us, planted from previous experiences of trauma, chaos, and dysfunction; when triggered, these pain points cause a heightened emotional response. Many of us feel shame and embarrassment around this experience, but what would it look like to accept and manage it instead?

Let's start here: You're allowed to feel your pain in this deeply painful world. You're allowed to have emotions about this complicated existence. Rather than denying your emotions, acknowledge and accept them, giving yourself permission to feel whatever comes along with life.

We often try to show up with a brave face and a shield of armor around us. But when life throws you for an emotional loop, know that this is not an indicator of weakness. Rather, these are moments to return to your practice of connecting with yourself, to bring forth your inner strength, and find your unshakable foundation within.

Remember, **don't be afraid of your emotions and reactions. Breathe through them and trust yourself.**

FIND COMFORT IN THE DISCOMFORT

Dear friend,

It's hard to step out of a comfort zone, isn't it? It often feels safer to stay in the know, stay in control, and stay closed off from the scary unknown. Living this way keeps us guarded, for sure, but it also blocks us from so much magic in life.

Life is a beautiful balance of comfort and discomfort, of enjoying what makes us feel safe and experimenting with where we can push the envelope. We don't have to be afraid of what we don't know, and we don't have to avoid opportunities or new situations just because they feel uncomfortable.

How can you stay open to new experiences, even when you feel unsure? By practicing curious optimism. Rather than feeling fear for all that might go wrong, seek out situations with the hope that they might bring something new or teach you something that can change your life forever.

Today, if you have an opportunity to step outside your comfort zone, go for it. Who knows what good might be waiting for you!

Remember, **you can pursue things that scare and excite you. Listen to the whispers of your soul, and let those desires guide you.**

CULTIVATE AUTHENTIC HAPPINESS

Dear friend,

Through my work, I've had conversations with people all over the world. Whenever I've asked about desires and goals for life, most people express that they simply wish to be happy. I'm filled with an array of emotions when I hear this response. The simplicity of this wish feels so pure, but its elusiveness brings me sadness. It is our birthright to be happy in this life, so why does it feel so hard to experience it?

How does the thought of a happy life feel in your body? When you imagine it, who are you with and where are you located? Let your answers clue you in on the next steps you may want to consider.

For instance, happiness might look like having a little more alone time for reflection or revisiting an old hobby or calling your friends more regularly. Asking yourself these important, introspective questions about what happiness means to you can help you tap into your true desires. Knowing how you want to feel and where you want to be are cornerstones to cultivating true happiness. Ask yourself, *What does it actually mean to be happy?* Your answer is unique to you.

Remember, **you are the architect of your life. You can make choices and changes to align with your true happiness.**

MANAGING UNNECESSARY STRESS

Dear friend,

My childhood therapist was kind and understanding. She was consistently in tune with my pain whenever I shared my worries and concerns.

I will never forget the advice she gave me: Life is stressful, and it always will be. It's simply the truth. There is necessary stress and unnecessary stress, and the key to living peacefully is to discern between the two. Hearing this set me free and gave me permission to choose how I manage my stress.

Necessary stress is unavoidable. It includes the aspects of life that we can't change or control and that bring with them complicated feelings. Necessary stress shows up as nerves before a big test or worrying about fulfilling our responsibilities. So what does unnecessary stress look like? For me it's agonizing over what I can't control, like other people's moods or actions and needless conflict.

Today, contemplate each part of your life that brings you unnecessary stress. Is it a person, relationship, or environment? How does it feel to know that you have a choice in how you participate in those areas of your life?

Remember, **you have the power to choose how you engage and what you take on every day.**

IT'S SAFE TO DREAM AGAIN

JUNE 8

Dear friend,

If you've ever had a dream fall flat, you know the searing pain of disappointment. When someone or something lets us down and we feel that our dreams have crumbled to the ground, it can be hard to put the pieces back together again.

After experiencing my own share of letdowns, I realized that I had two options for how I would allow them to impact me. I could either let them make me bitter and uninspired, giving up on myself, or I could reorganize my thoughts and remember that a closed door does not define me.

I've learned to find meaning in my disappointments, choosing to grow because of them rather than shutting down. I've cultivated a deep sense of trust that nothing can take away my worth, and I owe it to myself to keep going. I have allowed myself to dream again. I've made life's challenges my building blocks, rather than a wrecking ball, and I have found a new sense of resilience, optimism, and hope.

If life has let you down, allow your feelings about it to flow through you, but know it does not define you. Don't let sadness or disappointment deter you from dreaming, because you always deserve your dreams.

Remember, **have faith that the blessings you desire are on their way to you.**

BECOME WILDLY OPTIMISTIC

Dear friend,

    A certain beauty and privilege come with stability and the status quo. Monotony and repetition can be a blessing of sorts. But as human beings, we also crave excitement, spontaneity, and surprises.

    Throughout the ebb and flow of life, it can feel challenging to maintain an optimistic or excited view of the future. Once we feel as though we've ticked all the proverbial boxes or achieved what's expected of us, normalness sets in and leaves us wanting more.

    You have the power to shift your mindset on the days that feel a little listless and uninspired. You can choose optimism, reminding yourself that everything you desire is just around the corner.

    When you believe something amazing can happen at any second, you have a renewed and deeper sense of hope. How might wild optimism and expectation change your outlook today? How might this new mindset restore your capacity for joy? Shift your thoughts and keep the faith.

Remember, **you never know when life will surprise you with unexpected joy. Maintain hope and optimism, knowing that all you desire is on its way to you.**

LOVE YOUR TIMELINE

JUNE 10

Dear friend,

    I'll be honest: I've harbored some resentful feelings toward my life's journey. My expectations of what I thought life should look like rarely matched my reality. And, as you can imagine, comparing my life to others' didn't help. Moving forward I knew I had only two options: Try to unapologetically love my unique timeline or spend my life frustrated because of it.

    I choose to love it.

    It's painful to feel like life is passing you by or like your desires have been forgotten. But here's what I know to be true: Your timeline won't betray you. Can you take in this truth and let it plant seeds of trust and confidence in your own timing? Can you learn to love the path your life takes you on rather than resisting it?

    I've found so much relief being open to this perspective and reinforcing trust in my timeline. If you struggle with your own timing, I want this relief for you too. Take a breath, knowing that your path is not wrong and you have not messed up. You're never too late, and there's so much goodness ahead of you.

Remember, **you are not behind. Your timing is your own. Hold on to the excitement of infinite possibility in each new day.**

JUNE 11

PRACTICE PRESENCE

Dear friend,

My mom often says the mind is a tricky customer. Meaning, it's not always easy to live with our unruly minds and the incessant thoughts we think. What's the solution? Consciously choosing to be present, from moment to moment.

This, of course, is so much easier said than done. We are constantly faced with distractions, anxieties, and ruminations. When we think about it, our minds are likely out of the present moment more often than not. Knowing that presence breeds power, how can you start to bring your mind back to the now?

With practice, of course.

Notice how often your mind wanders away from the present moment, and gently bring it back. It often helps me to think of our minds as a blue sky, and our thoughts the clouds. Focus on the sky and let the clouds effortlessly pass by. The repetition of this practice will strengthen the muscle of your mind over time, and you'll start to notice deeper focus and presence.

The life you desire starts with a present mind, rooted in the now. Practice presence today.

Remember, you cannot change the past; you cannot predict the future. The only moment when you can have your full power is now.

CELEBRATE THE WINS OF OTHERS

Dear friend,

Is there anything better than experiencing love and support from our cherished people? Our loved ones add immense beauty to our days, and great joy and strength come from knowing we have people we can rely on or laugh with when we need them.

Just as we desire to feel love and support from the people in our lives, those people should feel our love and support in return. So why not celebrate them?

Sometimes we prevent ourselves from celebrating the wins of others because of sneaky pangs of jealousy or envy. That's completely natural. What helps me move past those feelings and offer authentic love is knowing that other people's wins will never take away from my own. When you champion others, they will naturally want to do the same for you.

Think of your loved ones: What are you proud of them for? How are you grateful for them? Why do you admire them? Now, can you reach out to them and share how you feel? Commit to creating beauty in someone else's life today.

Remember, **there is room enough for all to win, achieve, and succeed. Honor the people in your life for their successes, and the same sentiment will be returned to you.**

JUNE 13

HOW DO YOU TALK TO YOU?

Dear friend,

Who is your biggest cheerleader? How does this person talk to you? How do their words make you feel? Now, think about how you talk to yourself—are you your own number one fan, or are you your own worst critic?

Despite some of our better intentions, it's easy to fall into cycles of negative self-talk and disparagement. Our minds can easily latch on to critical thoughts, and if unchecked, they can snowball into doom and gloom.

The good news is that you don't have to live at the mercy of your own negative self-talk; you have the power to change your tone and reinforce what is positive and true. Today, witness your thoughts just like you would a conversation taking place in front of you. Notice where your mind goes and what it says. With this awareness, you can consciously choose to be kinder to yourself.

How does it feel to know that you can lift yourself up rather than talk yourself down?

Remember, **you deserve the love and encouragement that you give to others. Be your own cheerleader today.**

HEAL AT YOUR OWN PACE

Dear friend,

Breakups are the worst, and after going through a particularly bad one, I embarked on a journey to come back home to myself. I thought that if I focused on healing and processed my emotions, I'd be good as new in no time. So I dived deep into self-care. I attended courses and workshops and prioritized therapy. I did it all.

You can imagine I was disheartened when my efforts didn't elicit immediate results. I soon discovered that healing isn't linear, and there is no solution for getting over heartache. I faced the uncomfortable truth that time and patience breed peace.

Despite our desires, there are no quick fixes in mending broken hearts, and there's no equation for finding inner peace. Processing pain is a unique experience that cannot be outsourced or easily bypassed. We must persist, from moment to moment, one step at a time, with courage and optimism.

Healing is the brave act of showing up for yourself, even when it's hard; give yourself grace.

Remember, **there is no timeline to healing. Process, grieve, and evolve at your own pace. Let your healing unfold in its own time.**

IDENTIFY SURVIVAL MODE

Dear friend,

Have you ever had the feeling that if you could just get through a particular day, a week, a month, or even a year, everything would start to settle down? We often think that if we can somehow make it to some arbitrary finish line, we will finally allow ourselves to rest. But we all know how this goes. One day leads to the next, that finish line passes, and we are still pushing forward; this is survival mode.

To combat the road to burnout, self-awareness is key. So today, check in with yourself and ask, *How's it going being me today?*

If you find yourself uncharacteristically irritable or grumpy, you might be entering a period of survival mode. Check in and assess whether your nourishing habits are taking a hit. If you're constantly exhausted and overwhelmed by your regular routine, this is a signal to take a break. So much of life is not in your control, but you don't have to live your precious moments in a state of duress and exhaustion. Take time for yourself to nourish your body, mind, and soul with the tiny joys of life.

Remember, you deserve to feel fulfilled and happy in life's regular moments. Choose nourishing habits and call back your peace.

THE POWER OF SIMPLICITY

JUNE 16

Dear friend,

We are accustomed to chasing more, more, more, but what if the answer is actually *less*? I've been learning to trust that goodness will always come and that I already have enough. I have access to the peace I long for, just as I am.

So much beauty can be found in simplicity. We know that life can change in an instant, circumstances can shift, and our lived realities can be turned upside down. The unpredictability of life can help us learn to rely less on the external world and more on the internal. Simplicity allows us to come back to ourselves and gain clarity about our truest desires rather than being caught up in the life of excess. Instead of more, we just need the right things at the right time. Living this way helps me feel lighter, freer, and more like myself.

Today, ask yourself, *Are there areas in my life where I feel the call to simplify and connect?* Notice how it feels to honor yourself and your space when you release the excess in your life.

Remember, **when you simplify and find fulfillment from the inside out, you can find a more holistic sense of happiness and peace.**

THE COMPANY YOU KEEP

Dear friend,

Choosing to spend your life invested in self-discovery is one of the most meaningful ways to live. Witnessing your personal growth and honoring the many versions of you is a powerful practice of reverential self-love.

In your journey of self-realization, you may notice that as you change, you also have to make changes with the places you frequent, the activities you participate in, and the people you surround yourself with. As strong and independent as you may be, you are influenced and molded by these people with whom you spend your time.

So today, ask yourself, *Who does the company I keep motivate me to be?* Pay attention to how people around you sway your outlook, impact your actions, and make you feel. Sometimes people come into your life for a season, perhaps to teach you a lesson, and other times they are with you for the long haul. Know that no matter which category they fall into, there is validity and purpose for all who enter your life.

———

Remember, **you are worthy of having loving, supportive people around you.**

LIVE IN THE GRAY

Dear friend,

Good and bad. Light and dark. Highs and lows. Life's dualities help us recognize what's truly meaningful in this world. But if we get stuck in these dichotomies, they can keep us from finding balance in the everyday. I call it "living life in the gray." Meaning, rather than living for the extremes, whatever that may look like for you (those big highs, those great moments), seek to find contentment and acceptance in the stable middle.

It took me a long time to recognize the power of that middle path. I would give all my attention to fleeting, dramatic moments and experience those high highs and low lows. The pendulum of my emotions would swing violently from side to side, when real inner peace stems from a slow-moving center.

Living life in the gray means accepting your life for what is. It means letting go of extremes and learning to be comfortable in the everyday. Today, if you find yourself in a place where not much is happening, embrace it: This is where growth, restoration, and peace can flourish in your life.

Remember, **so much peace, happiness, and fulfillment can be found in the everyday. Give yourself permission to live in the gray.**

HONOR YOUR COURAGE

Dear friend,

It's hard out there. I know that we both already know this, but admitting it to you today just feels comforting. It takes bravery to persevere in this unpredictable and overwhelming world.

When I tell you that you are brave, do you believe it? Can you feel it as true? In showing up for yourself and others, you're courageous every day, whether you recognize it or not.

A few years ago, I set an intention to be brave on a daily basis, and it completely changed my attitude. I felt different. I leaned in to challenges rather than shying away. I spoke up, said no, and exuded more self-confidence. This is everyday bravery.

Where can you show up for yourself and be brave? Brave to protect your peace? Brave to speak up to someone who crosses your boundaries? Brave to bet on yourself, even if it feels foolish? Look for small moments and take a chance. Keep strengthening your bravery muscle, knowing that each time you choose it, it will get easier to live bravely.

Remember, **being exactly who you are is an act of bravery. Honor the courage it takes to never let the world dim your light.**

ACCEPT THE GIFT OF TIME

Dear friend,

I was never the type of person to be too wrapped up in the aging process. But when I entered my thirties, with a few decades of life to look back on, anxiety and fear of aging crept in.

We can't hit pause on the passing of time. With every moment, we are getting older, and that in itself is a gift. Still, it can feel scary not to be in control of time, and it's tempting to resist it. Rather than spinning our wheels seeking to control the uncontrollable, can we look to accept it instead? Peace and power are cultivated when we choose to embrace the steady passing of time and learn to honor the present day for what it is—for the *gift* that it is.

You'll never have this moment back again. So rather than cursing the inevitable, how can you be open to the changes that come and enjoy the time that's been gifted to you? Today, honor your life and each chapter of it by living in the present moment, fully and completely.

Remember, **time is a gift; don't waste it by wishing to change it.**

REWRITE EXPECTATIONS

Dear friend,

Have you ever wanted something so badly that you could feel it in your bones? Those moments in life when a desire burns so much, it's impossible to escape? When you achieve what you want, the exhilaration is thrilling. But in those unfortunate instances when you don't, the letdown can be heart-wrenching.

You might have heard the saying "expectation is the root of all heartache." Consider whether that's true for you. Zoom out and assess the expectations you have in your life. Maybe they are for how people treat you, for the quality of your surroundings, or for the timing of major milestones. How often are you let down by your high expectations?

If we want to know both joy and peace, we must find a way to chase our big dreams *and* surrender our expectations, creating space for the unexpected. We can start to manage our relationship with expectations by choosing to live with a sense of trust and deep knowledge that life will not betray us, no matter what happens in the short term.

Today, actively encourage a feeling of peace and acceptance for life's happenings, regardless of the outcome.

Remember, **even when you don't have control over what happens, you can control your responses and reactions. That is your power.**

CHOOSE HEALTHY HABITS

Dear friend,

You are what you repeatedly do. Contemplate this: Are your daily routines and rituals serving your highest ideals for your life? Be honest in your assessment. We know that each day is filled with small actions that ultimately shape who we are. What kinds of daily choices are you making? Do you routinely feel connected with yourself? Do you know what parts of your life make you feel good?

Healthy habits are the cornerstone of self-care and preservation; they are opportunities to show commitment to yourself and your well-being. The practices you choose to fortify your mind, body, and spirit can support you in rocky times and be a steadying force in uncertainty. Feeling grounded and rooted in your daily practices infuses you with confidence and strengthens you against the headwinds that might come your way.

What are the practices that make you *you*? What practices make you feel most alive? Which ones bring you peace? Incorporate a variety of practices to honor the different parts of yourself so you can flourish and become your best, most integrated self.

Remember, **choose habits and practices that serve your highest good; this is real self-care.**

MIND GAMES

Dear friend,

When I was younger, I was an avid tennis player. I practiced all the time and was a pretty good competitor. My technique and capabilities were on par, but ultimately, what kept me from being a solid winner was my mental game. I let mistakes completely take me out.

Overcoming the emotions that would arise in matches felt insurmountable. My mental game completely sabotaged my physical game. It was a frustrating part of my younger life, but it taught me an important lesson I carried with me off the court. I've learned to ask myself, *How often are the games I am playing in my mind sabotaging my long-term goals and desires?*

Notice what competitive mind games you may be playing with yourself. When you're in your own lane, focused on what you want to create, you will always get to where you want to go. Simply take a breath and get back in touch with who you are and what you want—and make choices to satisfy those needs.

Remember, **stay in your lane and trust the process; your life is not a competition.**

LET YOURSELF REST

JUNE 24

Dear friend,

No matter how busy your life may be, you are always deserving of rest. This might sound like a big ask, and for many of us, it's often hard to find time for quiet, personal moments. But you are worthy of this time.

I know you don't need anyone to give you permission to take a pause and reconnect, but maybe you need a reminder to actually do it—to carve out the time and space to rest.

If you don't know where to begin, let's start small, together, right now. Close your eyes and take a deep breath. Feel the air fill your lungs. Notice how it feels to let the air flow out of your body. Now take another deep breath, and imagine that air moving through your body, filling every crevice and reenergizing you from the inside out. How does it feel to take this pause? These small moments matter, and they add up!

Can you find a few minutes for rest and connection today? Be mindful of how it feels when you take time for yourself.

Remember, **life is a marathon, not a sprint. You need time to fill your cup and charge your battery.**

BE THE VILLAIN

Dear friend,

At a pivotal moment in my life, after years of doing everything I could to be liked, I decided I was no longer willing to people-please in order to keep a toxic peace. I realized I'd rather be aligned with myself, my truth, and my life than be liked.

I felt great about this—until I put it into practice. When the people in your life are used to you trying to please them, they will notice when you stop. It's an unpleasant shift.

But you know what? *It's okay to be the villain in someone else's story.* I repeated this to myself every time I went against my people-pleasing grain and chose differently. I *felt* like a villain, but was I really? By *villain* I don't mean being harmful or hurtful but rather allowing myself to disappoint other people if it meant standing up for myself. It became okay for me to set boundaries and say no.

Where could you try standing up for yourself like this today? The benefits of standing in your power and what you believe in, and not catering to the demands of those you once aimed to please, far surpass any surface-level pats on the back for maintaining the peace.

Remember, **it's okay to be the villain in someone else's story if it means being the hero of your own.**

LIVING THROUGH LIMBO

Dear friend,

Have you ever felt like you were stuck in limbo? Not the fun party game but the agonizing in-between? It's one of the more excruciating phases of life—not where you once were and not where you want to be, but stuck somewhere in the awkward middle.

When we set a goal, we understandably want to see it come true instantly. We become filled with excitement, thinking of the possibilities of life, so waiting for our desires to come to fruition is frustrating. And sometimes limbo seems to last so long that we feel like we have no choice but to give up on the dreams we're working toward.

Don't give up! Today could be the day when all you've been waiting for comes to be—you never know! Either way, don't let limbo make you think it's not going to work out. Can you find meaning and acceptance in your in-between moments? Because, as we know, there is purpose in them too. The stages of limbo won't last forever, so try to embrace each moment, knowing that there is so much more to come.

Remember, no moment of your life is ever wasted. Commit to being present, trusting that each phase has deep purpose and meaning.

JUNE 27

THE POWER OF A PAUSE

Dear friend,

There's something beautiful about a slow, considered response. We all cherish that friend we can call late at night in a panic with a problem. The friend who thinks it through with us, asks questions, and searches for the right solutions—that's a good friend. By honoring our experience, they provide calm and clarity to the situation.

What would it look like to be this kind of friend to yourself?

You can bring the power of a slow response to your own life. You will be tested and challenged at times, and you might be tempted to react quickly in ways you regret. It's easy to do—leaping into action or speech, reacting in a way fueled by emotion and not reason. But when we are reactionary, we often add fuel to the fire of chaos and conflict.

Yet when you take a pause, even just a small one, to reconnect and understand how you want to respond, you build a strong inner foundation that you and others can trust in any situation. If you find yourself tempted to react in haste today, take that beat. A slow response is your peace and your strength.

Remember, **how you react to a situation is up to you. This is your power. Pause, reflect, breathe, and choose.**

CONNECT WITH YOU

Dear friend,

There's a chunk of my life I lovingly refer to as my "chameleon era," the period when I stopped at nothing to fit in and feel accepted.

Have you gone through a phase like this? Those young years of self-discovery can be confusing and disorienting, and without a solid sense of self, I willingly molded myself to blend into any situation. Eventually, I lost touch with who I was.

It's exhausting to shape-shift and filter our behavior through the lens of others, hoping for their approval. We think this will help us find a sense of belonging, but it just leaves us feeling out of place. That's because true belonging begins within.

You owe it to yourself to stop seeking external validation and instead learn to stand firmly in your own identity. Know your values and respect yourself, creating space for others to do the same.

Self-connection is critical to discovering a more fulfilled, aligned life. Today, get to know the real you by spending time with yourself, just as you would with a dear friend.

Remember, **you are the only one who knows what it's like to be you. That is your gift. Honor your life by becoming fully invested in and connected to it.**

JUNE 29

HONOR YOUR EVOLUTION

Dear friend,

Sometimes when we look back at our younger selves, we feel critical of who we were and the decisions we made. We cringe at our former selves and feel embarrassed over our mistakes.

Let go of the unnecessary cruelty for that younger version of you. How, you may ask? When judgment rises to the surface, remember that everything you've said and done, both good and bad, has led you to this place, right now. Who you are at this moment is a compilation of every good decision *and* misstep in life. Those old versions were necessary for you to become the wiser, well-rounded person you are today.

From moment to moment, you may not recognize your growth, but when you zoom out and reflect on various threads of your life, you can begin to witness how far you've come. Each chapter of your life holds meaning, so if you find yourself harboring judgment for a past version of you, seek to view yourself with compassion rather than disdain. Ask yourself, *How can I honor who I was and how far I've come?*

Remember, **each version of you has added to who you are now and who you will become tomorrow.**

YOU MAKE THE RULES

Dear friend,

Have you ever broken one of society's unwritten rules? I've noticed recently that I've broken a few I always thought I had to abide by. As I'm writing this, I'm in my late thirties, single, and without children. I'm no longer working in a corporate environment; in fact, I work for myself.

The younger version of me would have thought these things blasphemous. This wasn't part of the plan, and it doesn't follow the life equation I learned long ago.

My friend and yoga teacher, Tara Stiles, once offered up this question to me: "Who made the rules, anyway?" I felt immediate relief hearing her say this. For so long, I tried to live up to societal expectations, without asking if they were right for me.

Are there any unspoken rules in your life that you want to rewrite? Are your goals and desires what *you* want, or are they influenced by what you think other people want for you? You are the creator of your life, and you can chart a path that diverges from the expected one. Give yourself this permission and this freedom.

Remember, you're allowed to rewrite the rules of life to benefit the amazing, unique you.

POWER THROUGH REJECTION

Dear friend,

It's not easy building up the confidence and bravery to put ourselves out there; it can be scary to be so vulnerable. Placing our trust in the hands of others can make us feel out of control. So when we push through all those uncomfortable feelings only to be turned away, it's only natural to feel deeply pained, unwanted, and just not good enough.

If the doors in your life have been closed one too many times, don't let them deter you from your pursuits. A special grit and resilience build when we stay committed to what we want, even in the face of rejection.

If you're feeling defeated by all the times you've heard the word *no*, take this love letter as a sign not to give up on yourself and your dreams. Bet on yourself and keep pushing forward, knowing that you'll soon hear the *yes* you've been waiting for. Many possibilities and opportunities are waiting for you. Be excited and curious for what is to come.

Remember, you are never defined by rejection; what matters is how you move forward from it. Never give up on what you desire.

HOW TO MOVE ON

JULY 2

Dear friend,

Letting go of relationships isn't easy, even when we know they aren't healthy. Setting boundaries and engaging in no contact are great tools to help in this area, and both often bring healing and closure.

Yet I have a handful of people who have inflicted great harm on me and my loved ones, and setting boundaries and restricting contact didn't feel enough. So today I want to introduce another practice for your self-care toolbox, given to me by my therapist years ago.

For the people who no longer deserve a seat at your table, consider this visualization technique. Put them into a vault in your mind—this vault is never to be opened, and they are never to be released. Imagining the harmful people in my life this way has given me a surprising level of relief and peace. I feel comforted in knowing that it is in my power not to let them come back, and this power fortifies me.

Would this practice benefit you? Are there people in your life you'd like to put in your own vault?

Remember, **not everyone deserves a seat at your table. You get to choose who stays and who leaves.**

DEFAULT TO UNDERSTANDING

Dear friend,

Is there any better feeling than being in the presence of another and experiencing that deep, authentic awareness that they *get* you? And on the flip side, when that's missing in a relationship, you might feel misunderstood or alone.

Practice staying present and open to growing in your compassion for and understanding of other people—even if you don't *get* one another just yet. Understanding and respect can be such beautiful precursors to deep connection and, ultimately, peace.

While it can be challenging to reconcile how different we all are, rather than picking apart our differences, could you look for ways to bridge the gaps between yourself and those with whom you disagree? Can you commit to leading with curiosity and respect, even if your first reaction is suspicion or judgment? With understanding as your default setting, you might find more relational harmony with others in your life. And you will be setting the precedent for how others should see and treat you.

Remember, **be open to understanding. It will bridge the gap that differences and disagreements create.**

FREEDOM FROM THE INSIDE OUT

JULY 4

Dear friend,

When you hear the word *freedom*, what comes to mind? Recently, I've found myself looking for a freedom that stems from inside myself. Freedom in mind, body, and action—those are the kinds of freedom that I want to embody. I want freedom from the inside out.

How can you free yourself from the thoughts that keep you entrapped? Finding freedom in the mind means noticing how you think and allowing yourself to choose differently, if needed. It means staying flexible and remembering your power to transform your self-talk.

How can you find freedom in your being? By trusting your body as your home and realizing that your body does not deserve the judgment, disapproval, or self-hatred you've been taught to place on it. It means letting yourself love your body, honor your body, and have gratitude for all it can do.

What does it mean to find freedom in your actions? It means exercising your power to change course whenever you need to. It might mean embracing exploration, staying open to spontaneity, and allowing yourself to do things differently, as needed.

Remember, **there are many ways to find freedom in your life. Explore what freedom means to you.**

IDENTIFY SILVER LININGS

Dear friend,

It's easy to view our experiences as black or white, good or bad, with not much in between. When we receive negative feedback or experience difficulty, it may be tempting to paint ourselves as flawed or unworthy.

As we know, we cannot live a perfect life; we will make our fair share of mistakes. Rather than beating ourselves up for our errors and spiraling in judgment, we can adopt a spirit of curiosity, leaning in to learn what our mistakes may be telling us. Be on the lookout for the silver lining of every situation. Just because something is hard, that doesn't mean it's all bad or that it doesn't have value.

As you reflect on even the darkest moments of life, ones where you struggled to find hope, you'll usually find a sliver of meaning rising to the surface. At the very least, you wouldn't be the person you are today without that experience. Think of how you've grown and all you've learned; your newfound wisdom is a gift you've gained through adversity.

Today, look for the silver linings, and know that no moment is ever wasted.

Remember, **there is more to your story, and there is always a silver lining if you look for it.**

OWN YOUR WORTH

JULY 6

Dear friend,

How often do you feel worthy? I'm talking about an unshakable sense of worth deep in your bones.

It's not always easy to be attuned to our worth, especially when the world around us chips away at it on a regular basis, making us feel like we must earn love or prove our value. We may have somehow received a message that we aren't enough or that we don't matter.

You don't have to live at the mercy of the world's messaging. Counteract the noise and remember what's true: You are always worthy.

Why do we spend so much of our precious time and energy seeking validation and acceptance without recognizing that what we desire is already within? You entered this world complete and enough. Chances are, it's the thoughts, opinions, and judgments you've experienced since then that have etched away at your internal knowledge of this truth. But the fact that you are living this life, at this moment, proves your value. So do not lose sight of your worth today. Own it, for it is already yours.

Remember, **the fact that you are alive means you are enough. Remind yourself of your inherent worth and act accordingly.**

RECONNECT WITH YOUR DESIRES

Dear friend,

For many of my younger years, the words "I don't know" were my daily affirmation. Making any decision felt impossible—from choosing what to eat to making big life plans. The possibility of choice felt like a burden rather than a blessing. I lived in a perpetual state of disconnect from myself and my desires.

Not feeling like we know is incredibly frustrating, both for us and the people around us. But it's understandable why we would feel this way. So much is asked of us every single day; it can feel overwhelming and exhausting to choose, so sometimes it feels easier to pass off the responsibility of choice.

Uncertainty and doubt often stem from a severance from our true selves. How can we possibly make choices and feel confident if we aren't in touch with who we really are from the inside out? Luckily, we don't have to live like this. We can reconnect and take ownership of our desires.

When you place importance on the relationship you have with yourself, you can know what you really want. You can experience freedom and confidence because you are finally living for you, on your own terms.

Remember, **taking the time to get to know yourself breeds freedom and confidence. You *do* know what you want.**

THE OTHER SIDE OF FEAR

Dear friend,

Do you desire more magic in your life? Or maybe it's more excitement or growth or fulfillment or opportunity. Is there something you've been yearning to try, but you feel afraid—of not being able to or not being good enough?

Let's talk about a simple shift that can help make your dreams possible in your life. First, if you feel frustrated by being stuck in fear, know that you're not alone. Facing what we fear isn't easy; we all go through this.

But let me encourage you to ask yourself, *What would I do if I wasn't afraid? Who would I be? Where would I go? How would I feel?* Do the answers to these questions excite you? Do they inspire you to try something new? Your soul may be whispering something to you that it's begging for you to hear. What would it take for you to step beyond your fears and follow your dreams? What life is waiting for you on the other side of fear?

Remember, **the magic in life exists on the other side of fear. Don't be afraid to go outside your comfort zone and discover infinite possibilities.**

IT'S OKAY TO STRUGGLE

Dear friend,

Though we all will move through our lives with different people, places, and circumstances, the bittersweet truth is that none of us will go through life unscathed. Even though we know that each of us will experience hardship, it's still tempting to blame ourselves for challenges that we face. You might tell yourself the lie that if only you were good enough, smart enough, or prepared enough, you could have prevented sorrow from knocking at your door.

Take heart that you are not wrong or broken because life has been harsh with you. Struggle is a natural occurrence of life. Release the need to hold yourself responsible for the things you can't control.

Rather than seeking to rid yourself of difficulty and pursuing the impossibility of a life without suffering, lean in to challenges with the inner strength and resilience you've built. Life isn't always easy, but your struggles will ultimately nudge you to learn and grow. And difficult times don't last forever.

Remember, **the bumps in the road of your life don't impact your worth. It's okay to struggle. You might bend, but you won't break.**

LET PEOPLE EXPERIENCE CONSEQUENCES

JULY 10

Dear friend,

Here's a tricky question: How often do you let the people you love take responsibility for their actions? It might seem easier to take the blame for someone's mistake or not enforce boundaries when behavior feels disrespectful.

When we do this, we often think we are being that kind, loving person we intend to be, but in reality, we are blocking others from experiencing the repercussions and teachings of their actions. Consequences are pathways to growth. Be open to the lessons that stem from mistakes. When we embrace responsibility for a misstep, we grow. We are changed—and for the better. We are honoring every aspect of ourselves, even those parts we aren't very proud of.

With that in mind, it's a disservice to let people off the hook when they don't deserve it. By avoiding hard conversations and brushing things under the rug, we take away the opportunity for someone else to grow.

You don't have to give passes for bad behavior. Learning this will change how you relate to others in your life. Today, don't be afraid to let people have their consequences, just as you embrace your own.

Remember, **setting boundaries and allowing consequences will help you become the person you are meant to be.**

JULY 11
YOU CAN'T MAKE OTHERS HAPPY

Dear friend,

"I just want to make you happy." "I want whatever you want—whatever will make you happiest." I used to love hearing these platitudes from people. I thought these were loving, caring sentiments geared to elevate my happiness. And I thought I could do the same for others by offering these words back to them. But is that even possible? Should I do whatever it takes to make someone else happy? Is that my job?

The answer is a resounding *no*.

Living to elicit an emotional response from someone else is a hidden manipulation technique, and it's also not possible or realistic. You can't force people to feel something, and honestly, you shouldn't try. As a kind, caring person, you can be a positive influence in other people's lives, but you can't change their emotions.

You can't make other people happy, and it's not your job or responsibility to do so.

Your loving presence and influence are always enough.

Remember, it's not your responsibility to manage the feelings of others. But you can show up for them and love them without expectation or judgment.

EMBRACE WHERE YOU ARE

JULY 12

Dear friend,

Have you noticed that as kids, we can't wait to be adults, and as adults, we yearn for childhood and youth? It seems we spend a lot of time resisting reality, fantasizing about an alternative. It's that "grass is always greener" mentality, and while it's tempting, it's an emotional drain.

A key to embracing the present is remembering the purpose of each small moment that we've been through. Our lives are like the building blocks we played with as kids—from the bottom up, we build and create our masterpieces. But like everything else, it is a process, and the process of becoming is not to be rushed.

Today, connect with and appreciate the chapter you are in, honoring every moment that has brought you to this place and holding space for who you will become. If you find yourself wishing away your time or yearning for the past or the future, why not pause to find that deep confidence in who you are right now?

Remember, **each moment of your life is precious and meaningful. Honor exactly who you are today and every day.**

JULY 13

WHEN TO MAKE CHANGES

Dear friend,

Years ago, when I was in a transition period, I was talking to a loved one, hoping to find some support and insight. My friend's advice to me transformed how I viewed the uncertainty I felt around change. "When it is time to make the decision," she said, "you'll know exactly what to do. If the decision isn't clear, it's not time to make a change."

This advice affected me in two ways. First, it was the exact reinforcement I needed to remember that the answers I need for my path are always inside me. When we are skeptical or when something feels "off," we can trust our gut. And second, I was reminded that we cannot rush life's timing.

It's true that we can have desires and affect our destiny through our choices, but this truth is balanced with the fact that there is a right time for everything. So much power comes in waiting for the answers we seek rather than rushing past them.

If you have perplexing choices or life changes in front of you, let me give you the same encouragement: Don't worry. You'll know exactly what to do. If you don't, wait until you do.

Remember, **trust in the purpose of each moment, trust your gut, and know that everything is unfolding as it should.**

BECOME TRUSTWORTHY

Dear friend,

If we want to have relationships and interactions that make us feel loved, fulfilled, and understood, we need to lead with trustworthiness. Relationships are two-way streets. It's not enough to focus outward on what we want from other people; we must also look within to see what we bring to the relationship.

So what does it mean to be a trustworthy person?

Trustworthiness means being honest but also being kind. Relationships that lack compassionate honesty lack trust. It means we communicate clearly. Life is much easier when we can kindly state our needs, wants, and desires to the people around us, and this takes away the space for guessing games, confusion, and mistrust.

Trustworthiness means being reliable. Trust is chipped away when our actions don't match up with our words. It also means setting boundaries. The most trustworthy people are the ones who know how to set boundaries and stick to them. If you don't know what you stand for, as the old saying goes, you'll fall for anything.

Lastly, trustworthiness also means being real. Be understanding, empathetic, and authentic. People love to feel safe enough to be vulnerable. This begins with you knowing exactly who you are and what you want.

Remember, **building trustworthiness is a practice that will open doors and bring the right people into your life.**

JULY 14

JULY 15

MOTIVATE YOURSELF

Dear friend,

You might be like me and love to indulge in inspirational content and materials. I've always been a seeker of knowledge, wisdom, and insights. I love to learn and am always eager to digest new information.

At times, I've taken this to an extreme. If there was an inspirational event, I was there. A new book? I bought it. A retreat? Sign me up. I was so hungry for any sort of information that could help me better live my life that it became all-consuming.

Today, I want to remind both of us that, yes, we can be motivated and inspired by gatherings and the wisdom of others. We can learn and grow from great mentors, and we can also find inspiration from within.

How can you inspire yourself? This practice is twofold: First, remember to stay optimistic, and second, remind yourself that everything you need is inside you, always. You don't have to seek out external forces of inspiration; *you* are an inspiration.

Remember, **you are an inspiration all on your own. Your own brand of magic and positive energy can help you move mountains.**

THE CHAPTERS OF YOUR LIFE

Dear friend,

We all have high standards and aspirations for our lives. We want to know that our hard work and wise choices matter; we want to feel at peace. Sometimes the intensity of our desires can lead to self-judgment, frustration, and harsh criticisms when we feel like our stories aren't unfolding the way we planned them.

Can you relate?

If so, try zooming out and gaining a wider perspective. Every story has a beginning and an end, but it's what happens between those benchmarks that matters most. The ordinary moments build character and help define who you are. Your story will have highs and lows, peaks and valleys, each part important and meaningful. Trust that each success and adversity is making you *you*. If you don't like where the story is going, you have the power to write your way out. You hold the pen.

If you're feeling anxious about today, try to view this moment as just one chapter in your life's grand story; it won't last forever, and it will serve a purpose. Trust that today's plotlines can ultimately lead to the resolutions and happiness of tomorrow.

Remember, there is no one in the world like you. Your story is uniquely yours, and no matter what chapter you're in, every day is an opportunity to turn the page.

JULY 17

YOU KNOW WHAT'S RIGHT FOR YOU

Dear friend,

How do you make big decisions? What resources do you turn to? When I've had to make an important choice, I used to poll everyone in my life, make a pros and cons list, and toggle back and forth in my mind about what was the right move. And to be honest, it felt like torture. I didn't think I could trust my own judgment and, thus, always sought the advice and opinions of others.

Over time I've realized that by relying so much on the insights and impressions of other people, I was completely negating my own. I was letting other people's preferences and tastes cloud my instincts.

So often when we face a fork in the road, we turn outward to find the right answer. Today, I want you to know that the answer you seek may very well be within you.

Of course, it's beneficial to share with and learn from mentors and loved ones. It's helpful to collect facts and inspiration and insights you didn't have before. None of us can get through life alone. But ultimately, other people's opinions carry other people's energies, so stay on course with what's true for you.

Remember, **you have a great deal of wisdom within you. Listen to it, and let it guide you.**

THE POWER OF PRESENCE

Dear friend,

You face hundreds of distractions and are pulled in countless directions every moment of the day. You may feel like your mind has been splintered, never quite knowing where to land or how to focus. Distraction is one of the most indirect but powerful obstacles we all face.

There's a simple antidote to this: Redirect your focus to what's in front of you.

This is called *presence*, and it's one of the most life-changing tools that will help you along your path. When you consciously pay attention to the moment, you can find deeper connections with others, become better in your work, exhibit more patience, and navigate the world with enhanced clarity. Presence is the simple but powerful practice that can change everything.

If you find your mind wandering today, robbing you of the present moment, take a deep breath and focus on the now. Observe where your mind goes, be grateful for everything around you, and see how being present can shift your whole perspective.

Remember, **you are the witness to your extraordinary life; be present and cherish every moment of it.**

EMBRACE COMMITMENT

Dear friend,

I used to be terrified of commitment. This might have been a trauma response or coping mechanism, but I never wanted to be tied down. I always wanted an escape plan. Life-altering commitments like accepting a job, signing an apartment lease, or even writing this book filled me with dread. I looked for excuses to say no or back out.

What I learned from this frustrating pattern is that you really can't get anywhere if you avoid commitment. I've started asking myself, *What if commitments don't have to be so scary? Is there a way to reframe them as exciting and life-affirming?*

We often avoid commitment when we aren't clear on what we want, which is why it's important to regularly tune in to our innermost desires and deeply held values. When we are confident in our goals, it's easy to say yes to them.

Is there a commitment you've been avoiding, afraid to jump in? Assess whether it's in line with what you most want, and if it is, trust yourself and your instincts and embrace the opportunity to go for your goals.

Remember, it's empowering to choose yourself and your dreams. Don't be afraid to say yes.

SHIFT INTO ACCEPTANCE

Dear friend,

People can be enigmas. It's easy to get caught up in wanting to know why people say and do the things they do, and it often makes us feel stuck and confused, swirling in uncertainty. You can really work yourself up, fixating on the behaviors of others—or even worse, trying to change them.

If you want to protect your peace, you have to accept people for who they are and remember that everyone is doing the best they can with what they were given. This mindset helps me approach others with forgiveness and understanding and allows me to live more harmoniously with those around me.

You cannot live the lives of your loved ones. You cannot make their choices, and you cannot assume responsibility for their actions. Release yourself from that role. Accepting people where they are means letting go of judgment and expectation; it means humbly respecting the fact that we will never fully know what it's like to be someone else. We've all been given different lots in life, and how we handle them will be different. Without compromising your boundaries or denying your values, you can release the need to fix or control and shift into acceptance.

Remember, **when you accept others as they are, you give them space to find their own path and learn their own truth.**

JULY 20

STOP FIGHTING FRUSTRATION

JULY 21

Dear friend,

Frustration can turn me into a Tasmanian Devil of irritability, spinning my wheels in chaos, leading me nowhere. Living this way for too long leads to burnout and exhaustion. But I've learned to ask myself, *What can frustration teach me when I stop fighting and resisting it?*

Beneath the surface of frustration lies useful information for your life. You can ask yourself, *Why am I feeling blocked in this moment? Am I pushing too hard in the wrong direction? Am I holding on to unrealistic expectations? Am I engaging in perfectionism to a degree that could produce only failure?* In stillness and openness, you can unearth important information to help guide you forward.

Can you embrace frustration today, knowing that it, too, has purpose? Frustration can signal where you have opportunities to make tweaks and shifts and can show you when it's time to consider a major life transition. Frustration can be the motivation you need to make the changes you want. But you must be open to it.

Remember, don't push away the feeling of frustration. It might be guiding you toward an action that can change your life's course for the better.

LET GO OF GUILT

Dear friend,

The idea I want to share with you today might sound a little controversial. Here goes nothing: Guilt is a useless emotion. I believe this wholeheartedly and hope to convince you as well.

I've spent so much of my life riddled with guilt, wishing I could go back in time and make different choices. I've agonized over what my life could have been, had I done things just a little differently, had life unfolded in a different way. But the agony and guilt I felt were useless, a waste of my energy.

No one can go back in time and do things over. So why do we spend our time trying?

Spinning your wheels in guilt only drains your energy and keeps you from doing the good you desire with your life. You can choose, instead, to focus on what you can do right now, in the present. You have the power to use the lessons life has given you and act accordingly. Find freedom today from guilt, knowing that the lessons of the past can be a trusted guide for your present and future.

Remember, **you don't have to spend your precious time riddled with guilt. Refocus your energy in the present and move optimistically into your future.**

CHARGE YOUR BATTERY

Dear friend,

I once accidentally left my mom's car door slightly ajar overnight, completely draining the battery. The following morning was chaotic, as you can imagine; we had places to go, and a dead car battery was getting us nowhere fast.

I like to think that humans are just like car batteries—but with more personality and flair, of course. We can't be expected to be perpetually on, to be perpetually without rest. We can't sustain it; our batteries will deplete. We are often told that the constant grind is the only way to success. But repeatedly pushing yourself past your limits will inevitably lead to burnout and fatigue. There must be a better way.

If you're finding yourself low on charge, can you identify places where you can pull back and replenish what you've lost? Can you identify practices that help you feel reenergized and renewed? Look at your schedule today and see if you can carve out time for your own restoration, or find moments throughout your day to close your eyes and simply breathe. Know that there is time for work and for rest. The life balance you crave starts with restful self-care.

Remember, **you need and deserve time to rest, recharge, and recover. You are not meant to be perpetually on.**

REMEMBER YOUR POWER

Dear friend,

One of the greatest truths that has impacted me personally is knowing that I cannot control anything in the external world. I can't control you; I can't control the environment or the world around me; I can't control life and its happenings.

This used to make me feel so small and insignificant. It used to make me feel powerless, until I embraced this simple shift in thought: Remembering what I can control reconnects me to my power.

I can't control the world, and in truth, I don't want to. But luckily for all of us, there are some things in life we can control: our responses, our reactions, and our energy. Whatever happens outside of our lives, we can manage our next choice, our next word, our next move.

No, we can't predict the things that will happen to us, good or bad, but we can develop a keen awareness and connection with ourselves, allowing us to respond to whatever life brings with grace, kindness, and peace. This is our power.

Remember, **in a world that makes you feel powerless, your ability to choose your next move can never be taken away.**

JULY 25

YOU ARE EASY TO LOVE

Dear friend,

Likely, there have been situations and relationships that made you feel like you were difficult to love or, even worse, that you were flat-out unlovable. If you've ever been in this position, know this: No matter what, you are inherently worthy of love. Let that sink in. How does it feel to know this as truth? When you finally make this your reality and live proudly in this truth, you may feel like a great weight has been lifted off your shoulders.

We all want to feel loved and valued by the people in our lives. There's no greater feeling than knowing we're seen, loved, and understood. So if someone has led you to believe you are unworthy of those things, I am so sorry, friend. You don't deserve that.

Soak up all the love you have in this moment, seeking it out in all the corners of your life. Reaffirm your unshakable ability to be loved and your faith that the people who will love, honor, and cherish you will make their way to you. No one and nothing in life can take away from your capacity to love and be loved.

Remember, **you are always worthy of love and care. Never settle for less than you deserve.**

GIVE YOUR THOUGHTS A HOME

JULY 26

Dear friend,

Wouldn't it be nice to escape from the noise inside our heads? Just switch off for a bit? Though it's not possible to rid our minds of thoughts, we can give the ones that aren't serving us a happy place to go. This is the power of journaling.

Think of it this way. When you have a long list of things to do, what happens? All your responsibilities replay on a loop: *Don't forget to stop by the grocery store; remember to feed the cat.* How do you manage this? You create a to-do list, so you can be confident that you've captured everything in one place. This releases the tight grip in your mind and frees your brain to accomplish other tasks.

Journaling your deep thoughts and emotions serves the same purpose. We all have thoughts that swirl in our minds, creating unnecessary stress and anxiety. Why? Because they don't have a home, so our minds won't let them go. Give yourself the space and grace to release your mind from all the thoughts that aren't serving you, and give those thoughts a home in your journal. Notice how much energy, clarity, and relief you feel when you start this practice.

Remember, **when you give your thoughts a home, you create space for confidence, clarity, and peace.**

STRONG FROM THE INSIDE OUT

Dear friend,

We know how important it is to seek knowledge and wisdom about the world around us, but it is equally as important to turn our focus inward. What wisdom might you uncover if you chose to know yourself in a deeper, more meaningful way?

Today, seek to meet yourself, just like you would a stranger for the first time. Ask yourself questions and be present to the unique qualities and traits that make you *you*. Spend time with yourself in silence and listen to the whispers of your soul. Be present to your emotions as you move through your day. Your feelings and longings are data points guiding you, and they deserve to be heard.

As you connect more deeply with your inner self, go gently, cultivating kindness and compassion for the person you are. Accept that you won't always get everything right, and that's okay. When you commit to connecting with your emotions daily, you will become more grounded and stronger from the inside out.

Remember, **the knowledge you uncover through introspection is as important as learning about the external world. Create space to study who you are.**

PERMISSION TO TAKE IT SLOW

Dear friend,

A lot can be said for the adage that good things take time. Slow-cooked food, slow-growing gardens, the book-writing process—or creating just about anything—you can tell when quality time has been spent on something.

But if you're like a lot of people, you're asking yourself, *Who has time for that?* The fast pace of our world can make it seem like we must constantly be moving and creating—and quickly—in order to succeed and achieve. It can feel as if there isn't time for more slow-paced aspects of life, and we tend to seek out ways to increase speed.

Even though the world around us encourages instant gratification and impatience, can we break the cycle, knowing that there is beauty and purpose in allowing life to unfold in its own timing? Can we release impatience and doubt and lean in to trust and faith, holding tightly to the notion that our desires and creations will come to fruition? Give yourself permission today to be slow, intentional, and confident.

Remember, **your dreams and desires will take time. Trust the process and honor your vision.**

THE OPINION THAT MATTERS

Dear friend,

When presented with the hypothetical opportunity of choosing a superpower, I used to want to know what other people were thinking. As wild as it sounds, I thought that this knowledge would give me comfort and clarity in a world of uncertainty. Little did I realize that being privy to the thoughts and opinions of others would only bring me heartache and confusion. We just don't need to know these things!

Constantly fretting over other people's opinions, thoughts, and judgments can run us ragged and lead us to lose a true sense of ourselves. But hear this truth: You are not responsible for how people view you. You can't control people's thoughts and opinions, and you can't force anyone to like you.

If you're not responsible for what people think, what are you responsible for? You are responsible for the work you do on yourself, every day. When you place your focus on the internal work, building confidence and real self-love, the thoughts and opinions of others become irrelevant, because you'll realize that the most important opinion is the one you have of yourself.

Remember, **live in alignment with who you are and what you want. What other people think of you has no impact on your truth.**

BREAK THROUGH YOUR FEAR

Dear friend,

Healthy fear can serve as a protector, a shield, and a voice of reason. Irrational fears and fabricated stories in our minds, on the other hand, run us ragged, take hold of our lives, and rob us of our peace of mind.

So ask yourself, *Where does fear have an unhealthy hold on my life?*

Think of something you really want: a big dream, a lofty goal, or a hidden desire. What's blocking you from pursuing it? Maybe you're afraid of judgment, rejection, or failure. These are unhealthy fears. And if these are why you're holding yourself back, ask yourself, *Is the denial of my dreams a consequence I'm willing to live with for the rest of my life?*

So much goodness, opportunity, and unexpected joy come when you break through your fears and use them to fuel you to the other side. Let's start today! Find the courage to face your fears of failure, of judgment, of rejection head-on, and uproot the thoughts of inadequacy that are keeping you down. Look your unhealthy fears in the eye, knowing they no longer have a hold over you.

Remember, **you are strong, brave, and worthy to live free from fear.**

JULY 31

FREEDOM FROM YOUR PAST

Dear friend,

If something is burdening you today, I encourage you to let it go. You don't have to carry around parts of your past that repeatedly drag you down. You can find freedom from the pain points that cause you to ache, even after so long.

It's easy to latch on to difficult moments and allow them to have a prime seat at the table. But those moments don't define you. The beautiful thing about our stories is that we get to choose how we write them. If there are parts of your history that add agony to your life, know that you can redefine the roles those moments play. A painful humiliation doesn't encapsulate the wide range of your abilities and strengths. An error in judgment doesn't capture your immense intelligence. A moment of miscommunication doesn't mean you can't connect well with others on the whole.

We all have parts of our lives that are painful and difficult. It's a simple truth. But we have the power to choose how that pain plays a purpose in our story.

What hard thing can you let go of, and what good thing can you take hold of in its place?

Remember, you decide how your past will impact your present story. What story will your life tell?

HOLD ON TO BEAUTY

Dear friend,

We've talked about so many ways to handle life's difficulties. But what happens when it feels like your tools just aren't working? What can you do when your efforts don't feel like they're enough?

Turn to the power of your imagination. A simple visualization prompt can often help when you feel at the end of your rope. Call to mind something beautiful, joyful, and loving. Really let yourself imagine it so intensely that you almost feel like it's real. Because, in some way, it is real. What you imagine has the power to elicit feelings the same way actual events in the external world do. My mom taught me this practice years ago, when my world felt particularly upside down. It became my lifeline when nothing else seemed to ease my anxiety. Keeping something beautiful in my heart and mind helps me recollect my peace.

What might this practice look like for you? Feeling gratitude for life's tiny joys: the air you breathe, the food you eat, the comforts you might take for granted. Focusing on the present moment and relishing in the significance of every second. Noticing the love in your life and feeling how much you matter.

What is something beautiful you can hold on to in your mind today?

Remember, **your life doesn't have to be perfect to be beautiful and meaningful. Be open to the small joys all around you every day.**

WHEN YOU FEEL STUCK

Dear friend,

Do you ever have what I like to call "blah" days? When you're not at your peak, and you're not in a valley; you're stuck in the weird middle. And that middle presents its own set of complicated feelings and emotions.

It's easy to look out for our emotional extremes, the highs and lows serving as benchmarks for our personal progress. When we feel like we're in the in-between, fear, anxiety, doubt, and uncertainty can start to creep in.

Friend, don't fall into the trap of emotional limbo. These mind games prevent you from going after the dreams you hold so dearly. They keep you stagnant and hold you back. Today, tell yourself that it's okay to let go of your doubt. It's okay to move forward imperfectly. As you do, notice what you tell yourself on the path of pursuing your goals, making sure to reinforce the good, the exciting, and the potential that is before you.

Remember, **your life deserves magnificence. You're allowed to encourage yourself to go after your dreams.**

SENSITIVITY IS A SUPERPOWER

Dear friend,

Many of us have been exposed to the narrative that sensitivity is a weakness. I felt so much shame for being sensitive—something I had no control over! It's just how I'm wired. I held judgment for the emotions that would rise to the surface in response to the world around me. I even believed that having these feelings meant I was somehow less-than, and I spent years attempting to push away this completely natural and normal way of being.

If you relate, let me reassure you that your emotions are not a hindrance. Having big feelings in a messy, complicated world is a normal human response. Your feelings are often clues to your priorities and indicators of what really matters in your heart of hearts. Being open and present to your feelings—no matter what they are, no matter when they come—is part of knowing and respecting yourself.

One of the hardest but most admirable things you can do is to be vulnerable and maintain a sensitive, empathetic stance toward how you feel and how the people around you feel. One of the kindest things you can do for yourself is to release judgment.

Remember, your feelings are a natural part of who you are. Pay attention to what they're telling you about yourself and the world around you.

REFRAME THE *WHAT IFS*

Dear friend,

Consider the *what if* conversations you have with yourself. You might not even realize you're having them, but these sneaky, anxious thoughts can take up much of your mental energy. This happens when your mind gets stuck in a loop, playing out the various possibilities and outcomes. It's easy to ruminate on all that could go wrong if you were to put yourself out there and go after your dreams.

The *what if* mindset has kept me in doubt and held me back from the things I was yearning for. This mindset drained my energy and chipped away at my self-confidence and self-worth.

We might not be able to stop the what-if conversations completely; they have a place and a purpose when we are mindful of them. But instead of thinking about what will happen if things go wrong, try flipping the script to ask yourself, *What if things go right?* What if everything works out for you? What if you achieve your dreams? What if you create the life you've always desired? Today, can you get excited about the *what if* question?

Remember, you don't have to place all your focus on what could go wrong. Today, imagine and be excited for everything that will go right.

LOVE PEOPLE FROM AFAR

Dear friend,

Do you feel a responsibility to maintain every relationship you have and to do whatever you can to make it work? Do you sometimes even tolerate bad behavior and disrespect, pushing aside your feelings for the sake of perceived peace? If this describes your experience, remember: You don't have to keep everyone close to have love and compassion for them. There are many ways to love people.

You're allowed to create physical and emotional space between you and someone in your life—even if it's just for a season, and even if you still love them—if your boundaries, self-care, and mental well-being call for it. Know that you can send love and care from afar. You can wish people well, hold them in regard, but still maintain your needed space.

When a difficult relationship produces distance, find comfort in knowing you're allowed to love people in your own way. Choose to love people from a space that is safe and healthy for you.

Remember, you can love someone and not be close to them. Give yourself permission to create distance, knowing the love you share is still meaningful.

BE A LIGHT FOR OTHERS

AUGUST 6

Dear friend,

    If you feel burned-out and overwhelmed by the division and energy of the world around you, you are not alone. We live in an intense time; it's not easy! Your feelings are normal. It's hard being human in such a messy world, and it's natural to struggle to find the light when the world feels extra dark. When you're in those moments, try not to be too hard on yourself, and remember that no feeling lasts forever. Everything is always changing.

    One of the surefire ways to lift your spirits when life has you down is to double up on your intention to be encouraging, compassionate, and kind. Kindness costs nothing, and to someone else, it can mean everything. Think of a time where your spirits were brightened and you felt empowered by a random act of kindness. When you feel down, receiving unexpected kindness can give you the fuel to power through. So if you're feeling overwhelmed by the darkness of life today, know that there is always light. Today, you can be that light for others with presence and care, emitting kindness for those who need it most.

Remember, **you have the power to bring light into darkness. No act of kindness is ever too small.**

YOU DON'T NEED APPROVAL

Dear friend,

You don't need the approval from people in your life—even people you love—in order to follow your dreams and chart your life's path. This is not to dismiss the support and love that come from others but to encourage you to build confidence in what you want.

Sometimes we hold ourselves back from taking action on the things we desire because we're afraid of judgment or rejection, or we're afraid that people simply won't understand. We dismiss our ideas and keep ourselves small.

But what if you didn't wait for that permission or approval before going after what you want? What if you followed your heart and pursued your desires? How would it feel to take action guided by intuition?

If there is something you've been yearning for, but haven't acted on out of fear or lack of support, know that so many people in this world are waiting to see what you have to offer. I'm one of them.

Remember, **sometimes you have to honor yourself so fiercely that you make choices other people don't understand. You will never regret showing up for yourself in this way.**

FIND MEANING IN YOUR FAILURES

AUGUST 8

Dear friend,

Let's face it: Failure is painful. There's no real way to mask the sting of unrealized dreams and unsuccessful efforts. But does failure really have to be all bad? Can some good come from things that have gone wrong?

Rather than viewing failure as a badge of disgrace, look at it as a symbol of courage and bravery. Failure is simply evidence of your efforts, an opportunity to be proud of yourself for putting yourself out there.

What else can we learn from failure?

Failure never defines your worth. It isn't a signal of your flaws but an invitation to reexamine and reconsider your approach. Failure is a lesson learned and wisdom gained. The things you failed at can help you grow and evolve.

Today, ask yourself, *What meaning and purpose can I find in my failed attempt? What changes should I make before going after my goal again?* By sitting with your failures, you might uncover a treasure that you otherwise would have missed.

Remember, **just because something hasn't worked out yet, it doesn't mean you aren't worthy of your desires. Keep learning and putting yourself out there.**

AUGUST 9

NOT EVERYONE HAS TO LIKE YOU

Dear friend,

When I was little, I carried the unrealistic expectation that people would always like each other. My young mind couldn't comprehend why they wouldn't. As you can imagine, this led to some uncomfortable lessons and painful heartaches. Whenever I had a disagreement or a relationship would end, I was completely baffled, asking myself, *What's wrong with me? Where did I go wrong?*

I developed a long-standing practice of people-pleasing, thinking that if I acted a certain way, I could gain approval, love, and acceptance. Years later, I finally had an aha moment, realizing, *It's impossible to make people like me, and that is totally okay.*

Not everyone will like you, and that has no bearing on your value, worth, or meaning in this world. On the flip side, ask yourself, *Do I like absolutely everyone?* I'm guessing the answer is no.

I've found so much freedom in releasing this need to water myself down to appease the masses, and in return I've found a deeper love and appreciation for myself. I am certain that the people who are meant for me will love, care, and accept me for who I am. The same is true for you.

———

Remember, **not everyone will like you, and that is okay.**

YOU DON'T HAVE TO WORRY

Dear friend,

If you were to take an inventory of your daily thoughts, how many of them would be dedicated to worry? For many of us, worry and anxiety would be the majority of our lists. We spend so much of our time thinking of all the things that *could* happen—and it's exhausting!

If you feel this way, you're not alone. Worry is a natural part of life. In fact, it can feel like life is set up for it. We live in a world of unknowns, tragedy, and disappointment. It's no wonder we're so concerned.

Today, gently challenge your inclination to worry. Has one anxious thought ever stopped your fears from coming true? Studies have shown that 85 percent of what we worry about never happens, and the remaining 15 percent, we handle better than we expected.[1] That's pretty good, right?

Identify one worry you're holding on to that you're ready to release. Can you open up to letting it go? Can you reaffirm what's good and true? Keep in mind that if any of it happens, you'll be equipped to handle it.

Remember, **you deserve to live in peace, free of needless worry.**

AUGUST 11

YOUR MOST PRECIOUS RESOURCE

Dear friend,

You have one precious resource in this life that fuels everything you do: your energy. What are you doing to protect it?

Protecting your energy looks like being intentional with your thoughts, words, and actions. It looks like discerning where to spend your time, choosing your battles, setting healthy boundaries, and saying no when necessary.

If you continually find yourself in cycles of burnout and exhaustion, this is a good sign that you're not giving yourself the permission you need to rest. It's a signal that you're overextending to meet the needs of others or to meet unreasonable expectations of your own, and you're consistently shortchanging yourself.

Ask yourself, *How am I protecting my energy?* If you can't answer this question with any kind of certainty, you might need to establish a restful self-care practice or two. You have only so much to give, and you are responsible for stewarding the resource of your energy. Honor yourself by taking authority over your well-being and actively protecting yourself from burnout.

Remember, your energy is your precious resource; be intentional to care for it in all the ways necessary.

PURPOSE IN PAIN

Dear friend,

I do not claim to know the extent of your suffering, but I do know it is part of your path. Sometimes we are faced with such deep pain that we start to wonder whether life is set up against us or if we are destined to suffer needlessly.

I used to live in fear of the next painful or traumatic event in my life. If things started to go too well, I would anxiously await the other shoe to drop. Over time, I realized that I don't have to live in fear of the future.

Our perspective on pain and suffering can transform its impact on our lives. I may not fully understand it, but I've come to see that pain is often a gateway to personal growth and revelation.

Pain encourages us to deepen our relationship with ourselves and foster greater awareness. It teaches powerful lessons that shift the way we view the world, and it helps us grow our capacity for compassion and understanding for ourselves and others. Pain often reminds us that we are never alone.

Today, give your pain purpose and let the wisdom you have gained light up your path.

Remember, life's challenges can always teach us something new. Let your pain build your strength, and trust that there is meaning in every hard circumstance.

AUGUST 13

START BEFORE YOU'RE READY

Dear friend,

That dream you've been putting off? This is your gentle nudge to go after it, even if you don't think you're ready. You put such care into your goals and desires, and it's tempting to believe everything must be perfect in order for you to be worthy and ready. But if you're waiting for the perfect set of circumstances, friend, you're going to be waiting a long time. Instead of holding out for perfection, know that you can start today.

So often we put our dreams on pause and delay our own gratification because we don't think we are capable enough or prepared to receive what we want. How many dreams are living on the back burner because we haven't felt good enough to go after them?

If there is a yearning inside you, let yourself go for it. The secret no one tells you is that people who achieve great things rarely feel ready. Today, join them—just begin.

Remember, you're allowed to follow your dreams and go after your desires, at any time. You are worthy of the life you desire. Start living it today.

NO MORE LITTLE LIES

Dear friend,

I often tell the people in my life that I can handle just about anything, so long as I am told the truth. This was put to the test when I discovered that in one of my closest relationships, I was constantly being fed tiny lies. Not because this person didn't care about me or had a malicious agenda—quite the opposite. They were trying so hard to make me happy that they felt they had to alter the truth to preserve my peace.

We went through so many conflicts because of this. While I know this person loved me, the small lies woven throughout our relationship left me feeling lost and disconnected. Through many difficult conversations, we created a pact of "no more little lies." We have intended to be so open to the truth that we know we can handle whatever happens when reality strikes. Good or bad, we are committed to honesty.

The truth isn't always easy, but it is the foundation for trust.

My mom likes to say, "Truth is the basis of all healing." And when I opened up to truth in my relationships, healing began. Let yourself find freedom in the truth, and encourage the people in your life to do the same.

Remember, **you are strong enough to manage the truth of life.**

AUGUST 15

BE GENTLE WITH YOURSELF

Dear friend,

Have you ever had all the information right in front of you—you *knew* what to do—yet you still chose incorrectly? Few things trigger self-condemnation quite like this. It's the worst, isn't it? I know the shame that comes with mistakes like these, and I've been so hard on myself for it.

Can I remind you of something? You cannot live life perfectly, nor do you need to. If you're maneuvering through challenges and difficulties, be gentle with yourself. Talk to yourself kindly. Take a moment to let the frustration pass, and remember that nothing is wrong with you. You're allowed to make mistakes.

It's not your job to have all the answers. Striving for perfection is not a meaningful use of your energy. Extend yourself grace and go easy on yourself for your missteps.

Today, think about the words you would say to a friend in your situation. What would they need to hear? Be that forgiving friend to yourself.

Remember, **even when you're trying your best, you won't get it all right. You are still worthy of love, kindness, and grace.**

RELATIONSHIPS CAN END

Dear friend,

If you're like me, you might have picked up the belief that every important relationship has to last forever. We want to be loyal. We value our shared experiences. And so, even when the relationship no longer feels like the right fit, we feel pressured to hold on to it.

But here's a truth to take hold of today: You are allowed to lovingly release the relationships that have run their course. The end of a relationship can be riddled with judgment—from ourselves and others. *Who is to blame? Was someone betrayed? Who is in the wrong? Why can't we make it work?* Questions like these might make you feel like you have to stay in a situation that just doesn't work for you anymore.

Not all relationships are meant to go the distance; some are meant for only a little while. Try not to catastrophize or criticize a natural occurrence of letting go. Sometimes we grow apart, and sometimes we have to say goodbye. If you're noticing that it's time for someone to exit your life, keep things in perspective. Your ability to love and be loved hasn't disappeared—it stays with you. Keep your heart open.

Remember, **relationships don't have to last forever to be meaningful, and a relationship ending never signifies your worth or ability to be loved.**

ONE OF ONE

Dear friend,

A palpable anxiety brews beneath the surface of life, whispering to us that we're running out of time or that we'll miss our big chance. As I've grown older, this whisper now feels like a scream. The benchmarks placed on me in childhood feel like they are passing me by, and I find myself scared, asking, *How do I measure up?* When I see someone else mirroring my struggles, I don't feel as alone. If I can find another person who matches my anxiety about the passage of time, I feel validated in my feelings.

While seeking shared experiences can help me find solidarity, it also subtly disconnects me from my self-confidence, as if my own lived experience isn't valid enough. It leads me to wonder, *Can I truly feel confident and centered in my life when no one else's looks like mine?*

In this question lies your work for today. It's an invitation to become so assured of yourself, your choices, and your life that it doesn't matter how your life measures up to anyone else's. *You are one of one.* This truth shouldn't make you feel lonely or singled out, but empowered and emboldened. Your path is yours, and your timing is unique. You are not behind. You are right on time.

Remember, **who you are is a blessing. Honor who you are and the life you're living.**

CREATE NEW GROOVES

Dear friends,

When I was in high school, I went through a difficult time with my best friend and was referred to a therapist for support. My friend and I had a falling out, and my thoughts were spiraling. I couldn't seem to quiet my perpetual negative mindset; I couldn't get out of my own way. But something my therapist said changed everything for me.

"Think of your thoughts like grooves in the brain. The more you engage a thought pattern, the deeper that groove becomes, and the harder it is to avoid. If you want to change your outlook on life, you have to conscientiously create new grooves in the brain by thinking new thoughts."

This description was perfect. I could picture exactly what was happening in my mind: The more I agonized about the situation, the deeper that groove became, and, ultimately, the harder it was to dig out of. I understood the importance of new thoughts and fresh grooves. It proved to me just how powerful our minds are.

Take inventory of what's going on inside your mind. Are your thoughts provoking creativity and optimism? Or are they reinforcing limited beliefs and negativity? Are there any new grooves you'd like to create today?

Remember, **you hold the ability to curate your thoughts. Consciously choose to create a nurturing, loving mindset.**

KNOW WHO IS FOR YOU

Dear friend,

For a long time, I had almost zero discernment over who had access to my life. If you liked me, you were in; it was as simple as that.

At that time, I had so little self-connection and understanding of who I was and what I wanted that it didn't really matter who was around me. All I knew was that by letting people in, I wouldn't be alone, and that's all I needed. Or so I thought. What finally woke me up to a need for change was the loneliness I felt, even in the company of others. I didn't feel love, support, and care, and oftentimes, I left interactions feeling depleted, confused, and overwhelmed.

Noticing how you feel while in the presence of others will tell you everything you need to know about your relationships. When you're with the core people in your life, do you leave feeling happy, understood, and at peace? Or do you feel tired, irritable, and uncertain?

Tap into your emotions and notice how people's energies make you feel. This can provide the information you need to make the right choices and changes when it comes to who you spend your time with. And it all starts with tuning in to you.

Remember, **your time and energy are precious. You're allowed to set boundaries around your relationships to maintain your well-being and your peace.**

SLOW IS PRO

Dear friend,

When I learned how to ski as a small, ambitious five-year-old, my instructor taught me an important concept: *Slow is pro.* This, of course, helped me learn to ski and not get injured on the slopes, but I've found it to be a useful idea to incorporate in my life even today.

We live in a fast-paced world that values speed over practically everything else. But I want to propose a different worldview: the power of slow. When you're slow in what you do, you can act purposefully and powerfully and have a greater impact. You can take time to tune in to your foundational beliefs and examine whether your actions align with your values. Slowing down helps you see life's beautiful subtleties that would go unnoticed at a quicker pace, and it allows you to extend grace more easily to the people around you.

You can stop. You can pause. You can go slow. You don't need to have everything accomplished right now. Take the pressure off yourself by rejecting the idea that the only valuable way to live is by achieving everything all at once.

Remember, **slowing down isn't a weakness but a strength. When you work with time, rather than against it, you find contentment and peace.**

AUGUST 21

FIND BALANCE

Dear friend,

If you're anything like me, you probably yearn for balance and equilibrium. But the semblance of steadiness, normalcy, and stability often eludes us. Is true balance possible in our complicated existence?

I think balance is possible, but we might need to reframe exactly what it looks like for our own lives. Often, we base our expectations or pursuits of balance on how it externally manifests for others or what we think we should need. The quest ends up adding more stress and even *im*balance. Other times, we are so tightly tethered to the idea of perfect balance that we leave little room for grace. Can you feel peace and relief today, knowing that the balance you seek is available to you—just maybe not how you imagined it? Can you be still and find equilibrium from moment to moment? Rather than constantly stressing about cultivating the balance perfectly, check in with yourself and see what you need most.

Each day offers unique challenges and opportunities; ask yourself what you can do for yourself that will bring you a more authentic sense of peace from within.

Remember, **showing up every day with an open mind and an open heart is always enough.**

YOU DON'T HAVE TO SETTLE

Dear friend,

I've often settled for things that were *close enough* to what I wanted. Subconsciously, I didn't believe I could have what I actually wanted, so I latched on to the next best option.

Over time, though, settling for people, places, and things that were almost good enough fed the belief that I was unworthy of my desires. Deep down, maybe I felt I didn't deserve them. I was frustrated with how my life was unfolding, but I didn't realize it was because of my choices, not my worthiness.

When I shifted my mindset, took responsibility, and stopped settling, I started making decisions that honored my desires. I may not have all the things I want in life just yet, but I feel content knowing I'm not compromising anymore, and that has made all the difference.

Ask yourself, *Do I feel worthy of what I really want?* If there's some doubt, see if you can uncover where it's coming from. You're allowed to pursue your desires, and you don't have to settle for anything less.

Remember, **your life is worthy of the prize. What you desire is on its way to you.**

YOUR POWER LIES WITHIN

Dear friend,

We don't have control over the weather. We don't have the power to make other people do what we think they should do. We can't fly or see through walls or move with super speed. All those superpowers we see in the movies are the stuff of dreams. But this doesn't mean you are powerless.

Your power comes from within—you control what you say and do and value. You control your efforts and your actions. You can prepare for whatever comes your way by knowing your values, articulating clear intentions, and setting boundaries for what you will and won't accept. This is power.

If you're ever feeling powerless, susceptible to the world's events swirling around you, it's important to pause and remember what you can and can't control. Though this practice is easier said than done, it will become easier the more you try it.

Take time to get an understanding of what is in your control. Reflect on your boundaries and practice communicating them clearly. Let go of the parts of your life that are not aligned with where you want to go. You have the power to do all this and so much more. Take a step toward using it today.

Remember, you always have power; simply know that it resides within you.

YOU WON'T BE LEFT OUT

AUGUST 24

Dear friend,

The fear of missing out—or FOMO, as we all know it now—was a huge part of my younger life. As I've gotten older, I'm less afraid of being excluded. Building confidence and trusting that I will always be in the right place at the right time have given me peace.

The fear of missing out is a trick our minds play on us, having us believe we're making the wrong choices and losing out on a better life. When we spend our time wishing we were somewhere else or with different people or doing different things, we rob ourselves of the ability to enjoy the present.

I broke out of this mindset by remembering the power of the present moment. I stopped imagining stories about what I might be missing and started writing better ones, rooted in my reality.

I hope you know that wherever you are in your life, you haven't been left out, and you're not going to be left behind. Believe and trust in your life path, and know that gratitude for the present is always a better option than worry or regret.

Remember, **have faith and confidence in yourself, knowing that what you have is better than anything you might be missing.**

AUGUST 25

A BEAUTIFUL MESS

Dear friend,

Do you ever allow yourself not to have it all together? Are you accepting of yourself when you're a little unpolished or feeling off your game? Do you embrace and even celebrate the messy, unkempt versions of you?

We usually desire to present ourselves in tip-top shape. We don't want to show our flaws and feel embarrassed about our perceived imperfections. We make mistakes and mess up and can feel shame. But do we really need to be so hard on ourselves for this totally normal aspect of human life?

The truth is, you are a multidimensional person with an array of characteristics that make you who you are. Just as your best qualities have value, so do your messy ones. It's all part of what makes you *you*.

Life would be so boring without our little imperfections and mishaps. Sometimes, it's in the mess where we find the masterpiece. You, friend, can be a beautiful mess today. You don't have to edit yourself or dim your light to please others.

Remember, **honor every part of you, messy parts and all, for making up the beautiful masterpiece that is your life.**

ANGER IS YOUR ALLY

Dear friend,

One feeling we often repress, or even fear, is anger. Do you ever avoid expressing your anger, pushing it down because you're afraid that people will perceive you poorly?

Depending on your upbringing and personal context, you may have been discouraged from feeling angry or even subconsciously denied the right. Many of us have been led to believe that being put together, being calm and collected, or being easygoing is more attractive or appealing. We've been taught to judge anger and fear it within ourselves. Today, let's ask, *Why?*

Anger has a rightful place in your life, just like every other emotion. Anger is a reaction to injustice, harm, and disrespect. Anger has the power to teach you about yourself. It can tell you what you really care about, but only if you let it.

Start to notice the parts of your life where you've wanted to be angry but held yourself back or pushed the feeling down. Create space in your life for anger and honor what it's telling you. Know that you're allowed to express your anger in a mindful, purposeful way.

Remember, **anger can be your ally and your friend. Tap into this emotion to find knowledge and power.**

BE WHO YOU NEEDED

Dear friend,

Our formative years shape so much of who we are as adults. Our beliefs, opinions, and perspectives are influenced by our upbringings and lived experiences. Inevitably, there will be some aspects of ourselves we will want to hold on to and others we will need to let go of and heal from.

Seek to be the kind of person you needed or wished for when you were younger. Tune in to the unmet needs of the past and choose to fulfill them now. Because, the truth is, you can't go back and change what happened, but you can heal those wounds.

Being who you needed may look like practicing patience, staying present, and affirming yourself of your worth. If there's anything you still need to hear, nurture yourself with those kind words. If you notice patterns you wish to address, take note of them with gentleness and care.

Trust that you are secure in the safety of your own presence, and remember that it's never too late to heal, never too late to grow, and never too late to find the peace you deserve.

Remember, you can find healing from your past in the present moment. Embody the qualities you needed then, and find love for yourself in the now.

HOPE FOR THE GOOD

Dear friend,

There's a reason people say, "When it rains, it pours." Doesn't it seem like difficult moments always pile up? We don't know when the rain will come, but when times feel especially hard, will you stay true to the course?

When the rain pours, you may feel tempted to throw up your arms and give up, wallowing in apathy. You may doubt the power of your efforts and your beliefs to make a difference. You may begin to believe that a "who cares?" mentality will bring relief. But in the long run, indifference will only prolong your hardship.

Can you commit, instead, to holding on to hope and optimism for the good that is to come? Can you trust that your challenges are only momentary?

If life has been hard on you, or the difficulties you've faced have left you feeling left behind, let yourself experience that sadness, but don't stop there. Even as the rain falls, let yourself open to the possibility of all the rainbows and sunshine to come.

How do you feel when you remember that each new moment presents a new opportunity? Let yourself believe something good is always on the horizon.

Today, it's closer than it's ever been.

Remember, **each passing breath is an opportunity for a new beginning. Hold on to hope.**

CREATE SPACE FOR GRACE

Dear friend,

Life is seasonal and ever-changing. What is this chapter of your life presenting to you? Are you holding yourself to high expectations and impossible standards? If so, give yourself a break today.

Despite knowing differently, maybe a part of you still feels that if you try a little harder, you can achieve perfection. You value your roles and responsibilities, and you don't want to let people down. But all gas and no brakes will leave you confused, tired, and disappointed.

What would your life look like if you released expectation and perfectionism? How do you think you'd feel if today you choose to show up to your life exactly as you are, unapologetically? What if you truly believed that your best is enough?

Releasing the need to have it all together, all the time, creates the space for grace. It allows you to have messy moments and feel "off" if you need to. Can you honor what you've accomplished and embrace your success without obsessing over what comes next? Are you willing to deprioritize some tasks, knowing you're a human being, not a machine?

———

Remember, **you're allowed to release yourself from any unrealistic expectations you've set. Let yourself be.**

MANAGING BETRAYAL

AUGUST 30

Dear friend,

Don't we all yearn for those relationships that bring mutual support and care? When we find them, we want to hold on to them as tightly as we can.

Meaningful relationships are rare, so when someone we love disappoints or betrays us, it stings. It breaks our hearts and diminishes our foundation of trust. And even when we think we've found the people who are meant to be with us to the finish line, we discover that none of us is exempt from disappointment.

Learning that your trust has been broken or realizing that someone isn't who you thought they were can be deeply unsettling. It's difficult to move through the feelings of betrayal, and it's even more difficult not to let these experiences harden you so that you shut yourself off from other relationships.

Remember that what other people do, how they treat you, and, ultimately, how they manage your trust are not reflections on you. Don't allow mistreatment in your relationships to define your worthiness for love and care.

Remember, **honor your open heart and your trust, and be open to those who will honor and respect you in their lives.**

YOU ARE LIMITLESS

Dear friend,

My mom bravely went into treatment for bulimia when she was twenty-eight years old. During inpatient therapy, she agonized over her future. She was incredibly type A and desired a life that was organized, well planned, and on track. Noticing that she was becoming tangled in her own web of perfectionism, her therapist asked her to consider a new thought process.

She told my mom that her viewpoint was too limited, thinking she had only two options for her future: plan A or plan B. How would she feel if she widened her imagination to include plans A to Z?

My mom credits this shift in perspective for changing the course of her life, and her sharing it with me certainly changed mine. Leaving treatment, my mom embarked on a forty-year path of studying mindfulness and meditation (and, of course, raising me).

Let my mom's story remind you that you have limitless potential. Today, open yourself to new possibilities and opportunities. Dare to ask whether you are limiting yourself by dreaming small or selling yourself short. What if you became open to the array of potential that exists for your life? What if you accepted your limitlessness?

Remember, **the possibilities for your life are endless; notice the ways your life can surprise you when you open your mind.**

SET HEALTHY BOUNDARIES

Dear friend,

I'll admit that I have a hard time saying no to people. I really, truly hate to disappoint others. So as you can imagine, people-pleasing comes naturally to me. I've said yes to things that were obvious nos. I've overextended and put myself in situations that were not in my best interests. And because of this, I have felt frustrated, overwhelmed, resentful, and angry.

One of my favorite experts on the topic of boundaries, Nedra Glover Tawwab, said, "When you feel resentful, look for the boundaries needed."[1] This changed everything for me.

Boundaries are the ultimate act of self-care. When I started to set healthy boundaries in my life, I felt more at peace and connected with myself and others. I no longer did things for the sake of being liked, but because I truly wanted to. And the people in my life felt and appreciated that.

Setting boundaries allows you to communicate your needs and create space for the people in your life to do the same. Give yourself permission to say a gentle no if you feel pushed beyond your limits, and notice how much better you feel.

Remember, **let yourself be open to boundaries in your life. Allow yourself to stand up for yourself and your needs.**

QUALITY OVER QUANTITY

Dear friend,

Society teaches that productivity is the ultimate measure of success. It's messed up, isn't it? I refuse to believe that human existence is meant to be defined by quantity over quality. And yet many of us fear being perceived as lazy and unmotivated.

Is it any surprise that this mindset is leading to high levels of burnout and exhaustion?

First, we aren't meant to live this way, so how can we fix it? We must start by changing how we derive our self-worth. Our value and right to happiness are inherent, not based on our ability to produce, earn, or create. What we do in our precious life is a bonus; how we show up and who we become is how we'll be remembered.

Rather than accepting the grind at all costs, can we seek intentionality with our actions? Can we prioritize self-care over productivity?

Know that the time you spend in stillness has purpose. Being unproductive has value too. Being present is a virtue. Lean in to the notion that your time is never wasted, and you are always doing enough.

Remember, **you have nothing to prove, you are always worthy, and you are enough.**

GIVE YOURSELF PERMISSION

Dear friend,

We are taught in our formative years to seek permission before taking action. As adults with free will, seeking external approval is no longer required. But how often do we subconsciously stop ourselves from making moves because we are waiting for someone else to give us the green light or stamp of approval?

Is there something you deeply desire, but you hold back out of fear? Are there thought patterns pushing you to believe you need permission to chase what your soul yearns for?

The good news is, you have the freedom and power to pursue your heart's wishes, on your own terms. You don't need approval to embark on something meaningful to you. Your permission comes from within.

Even if your choices don't make sense to others, know that this is your life to live. Go at your own pace; let yourself be different. Give yourself permission, trust yourself, and embrace all that you create.

Remember, **your life is your own; give yourself permission to live it in a way that's right for you.**

A NEWFOUND FREEDOM

Dear friend,

I won't sugarcoat it: Life is tough. I used to be in denial about the harshness of life. I thought that if I tried hard enough, I could find the magical cure to living with ease.

M. Scott Peck's book *The Road Less Traveled* changed my entire perspective with these words: "Once it is accepted, the fact that life is difficult no longer matters."[2] When we accept this truth, we experience a newfound sense of freedom.

As we come to terms with the challenges of being human, how can we better manage the difficult or negative parts of life? Can we strengthen our inner world to such a degree that bumps in the road no longer rattle us? Through commitment to self-care and with awareness, presence, and rooted confidence, I believe we can.

You can find freedom in knowing that you no longer have to seek to rid the world (or your life) of its challenges. Redirect your focus to accept what is, homing in on the actions you can take to help you feel more centered and at peace. It feels good living this way, doesn't it?

Remember, **you cannot escape life's difficulties, but you can manage how you respond. You've got this.**

NOT DEFINED BY MISTAKES

Dear friend,

When you were a kid in school, maybe you encountered a star chart—the one where you got a sticker for good deeds and lost one for bad behavior. For whatever reason, I let this scorekeeping creep into my adulthood. For years I kept track in my mind of the good and the bad of my life. I thought if I could keep my "score" high I'd be satisfied and successful. If I did enough good and as little bad as possible, I thought I'd feel accomplished.

Ultimately, this framework brought a lot of guilt and self-condemnation. I was too hard on myself for my mistakes, believing that they took away from who I was; that something was wrong with me.

If you, too, find yourself keeping score of your life, holding yourself to impossible standards, it's time to leave this mentality behind. Your deeds, both good and bad, don't dictate who you are. You are not defined by your actions.

Today, be empowered by your past and the choices you made. They got you where you are right now. Know that your mistakes paved the road for growth. Give yourself grace today and always.

Remember, no single moment defines the magnificence of your life. You can choose the narrative of your story.

REALIZE YOUR FUTURE JOY

Dear friend,

Sometimes it feels like a huge chasm exists between setting our goals and realizing them. So many factors are outside of our control on the path to achieving what we want most. The journey can be long and exhausting.

But that's the tricky dynamic to dreaming! We start out with a rush of excitement and possibility but get dragged down by disappointment when the timing doesn't match up with our expectations.

If your dreams haven't come to fruition yet, rekindle that passion you felt when you first imagined that big life desire. Now imagine what it will feel like when you achieve your success. Really allow yourself to feel, visualize, and imagine what this will look like for you. What does this look like? How does it feel?

Let this practice connect you to your feelings and fuel you as you continue to create. Enjoy the journey and the road to success. Wherever you are on the path, your goals haven't failed you, and your timing isn't against you. Feel pride today, believing that what you are working toward will soon be your reality.

Remember, **no matter where you are on your journey, you're allowed to feel joy. Don't wait for the destination to feel pride for who you are.**

SEPTEMBER 7

CULTIVATE INNER STRENGTH

Dear friend,

What does it mean to be strong? Usually when we hear this word, big, powerful muscles and physical capabilities come to mind. But today, I want to talk about a different strength, stemming from mental toughness.

If you desire to be strong and steady from the inside, you must put in the work, just as you would to build physical strength. Practices like meditation and mindfulness are like taking your mind to the gym. They are time dedicated to building your connection with yourself. When practicing mindfulness, you strengthen the muscle of your mind by training it to focus on the present moment, even with distractions, even when it wants to wander. Repeated action builds habit, which builds strength.

Check in with yourself and ask yourself, *Where can I carve out time to connect with myself today? How can I be more present and intentional with my time? How can I strengthen the relationship I have with myself?*

———

Remember, **knowing yourself deeply and cultivating inner strength are worthwhile endeavors.**

HEALED VERSUS HEALING

Dear friend,

How do you view the process of your own healing? Are you an active participant? Do you resist it or resent it? Do you perceive healing as just something else on your long to-do list? I ask you these questions so we can uncover important answers.

The journey of healing is important, always worthwhile, and necessary. But sometimes I think we lose sight of how it works. We often view healing as a destination to arrive at or an award to achieve rather than a lifelong process of fulfillment and growth. The truth is, life is difficult, and with every processed trauma, it's likely that a new one will present itself. Don't let the persistent nature of challenge dissuade you from making the effort to heal.

Can you start to view healing as a daily intention, a forever practice, or a mindset? Can you think of healing as an opportunity—to learn, to grow, or to deepen your relationship with yourself and others? Today is the start of a beautiful relationship with healing in your life.

Remember, **healing isn't a destination, and the time you spend healing, growing, and learning is never wasted.**

KNOW YOUR PERSONAL LIMITS

Dear friend,

Do you ever dream of boundless energy, infinite patience, endless resilience, and unlimited attention for everyone you meet? Do you ever wonder how life would feel if we were free from our constraints? It's easy to view our limitations as obstacles, holding us back from all we wish to achieve. But being human means having limits.

For a long time, even though I comprehended this intellectually, I was critical of myself, ashamed that I wasn't better or stronger or able to handle more. I would compare my bandwidth to others' and feel embarrassed by my need to say no. Over time, I've learned to love who I am and respect my own capacity. Just like with every part of life, what works for one person may not work for another. My boundaries and limits won't always look like yours, and that's totally okay!

How comfortable are you with your limits? Can you embrace them rather than resist them? Today, know that your needs are always valid, and the boundaries you set to support your well-being are important. You never have to apologize or explain your desire for self-care.

Remember, **it's not easy to commit to self-love and care. Know that you deserve respect and kindness, always.**

OWN WHAT YOU WANT

Dear friend,

As you know by now, decision-making has not always been my strong suit. The last day of my senior year in high school was college T-shirt day, an opportunity to display where the next chapter would take me. It was meant to be fun and celebratory. But steeped in indecision, I was torn between two options and hadn't chosen which school to attend. I was so embarrassed, it was agony.

So when the last day of school rolled around, I showed up that day in a T-shirt from one school and a sweatshirt from the other. And yes, it felt as ridiculous as it sounds. The major life decision of choosing a college trapped me with fear, doubt, and uncertainty. The disconnect from myself and my true desires exacerbated my indecision. You see, I hadn't yet recognized the *privilege* of choice.

If my story resonates with you, let this be a sign to release your fears around decision-making. Build on the trust you have in yourself and affirm that you know what's right for you. Imagine the freedom you will experience when you allow yourself to make choices confidently. Ask yourself, *What will I choose today?*

Remember, **your ability to choose is a great privilege; own that you know who you are and what you want.**

SEPTEMBER 11

LESSONS FROM LOSS

Dear friend,

While life is filled with magic, happiness, and joy, we know all too well that it's also filled with loss. Relationships end, situations change, loved ones are lost, and seasons of life come to a close.

There's no saying how the role of loss will play out in our lives; we can't predict the toll it will take.

Reeling from loss is hard and painful but is a natural part of life. If you're grieving someone you love or simply an old version of yourself, lean in to the sadness, because this is simply an expression of your love.

Start to think of the experience of loss, in any shape or form, like waves in the sea. The tides roll in and the tides roll out, but the ocean's foundation remains. Emotions rise and fall, and through it all, we persist. Rather than believing the loss we experience will break us, let's contemplate how it shapes us.

With resilience and perseverance, you can ride the waves of your emotions. You can find strength in yourself, knowing that you are capable of managing the tides. Losing one part of your life doesn't mean you've lost everything. Even as the waters change, love and honor always remain.

Remember, **loss, change, and sadness are natural parts of life. Learn to ride these waves with grace and persistence.**

POWER IN THE PIVOT

Dear friend,

It's a brand-new day. You can't change what happened yesterday, and you can't predict what will come tomorrow. But you have the gift of the present moment and the power to choose how to live in it.

It's comforting to know that despite whatever transpired in the past, you have the opportunity to begin again, to change direction, to make choices that will move you toward your deepest desires. Even if you feel stuck or weighed down by life, you can decide to shift your course.

If you're feeling a nudge to chart a different path or make a change, know that you can start today. Be present and open to your internal cues, listening to the whispers of your heart. Stay attuned to new opportunities and allow yourself the freedom to pivot from what was to what will be. When you are flexible with how you envision your life, you become open to so much more than you can imagine. Isn't it exciting to consider the possibilities when you live with this perspective?

Remember, **pivots can lead to hidden blessings. Be open to and curious about new opportunities.**

SEPTEMBER 13

NOT YOUR RESPONSIBILITY

Dear friend,

Sometimes, as nurturers, we take on too many responsibilities and overextend ourselves. We want to be the fixers, the pleasers, the ones who make life great for the people around us, but if we overdo it, we wind up feeling burned-out, resentful, and angry.

This shift can be insidious, sneaking up on you when you aren't paying attention and wreaking havoc on your emotions and energy levels. Keep an eye out for the imbalances in your life, for the times when you feel like you are constantly giving and trying, without notice or appreciation.

Today, can I remind you of what you're not responsible for in life and give you permission to let go of these roles? You are not responsible for

> managing other people's moods,
> living up to other people's expectations,
> taking responsibility for other people's actions,
> being the peacemaker or the fixer in your family, or
> changing other people.

Never forget that your presence is a gift, and you're in charge of how you share it.

Remember, **you can give, care, and nurture from a pure heart when you know what you are not responsible for.**

LET PEOPLE BE WRONG

SEPTEMBER 14

Dear friend,

Someone once gave me the most freeing piece of advice: "Let people be wrong about you. It's not your job to convince them of your truth."

This piece of advice has truly stuck with me. I used to feel that I had to put in constant effort to keep people in my life, almost as if it were a full-time job. Over time, I've recognized that not everyone I meet is going to be right for me, and I'm not going to be right for everyone else.

The "right" people will assume the best about you, not the worst. The right people will be compassionate, not judgmental. The ones who are meant for you will accept the real you and allow grace and space for you to learn, grow, and become. The right people will want to stay without expecting you to jump through hoops for them. You won't have to worry about proving yourself, because the right people won't need proof. And, of course, you'll do the same for them.

I want you to know that it is not your job to convince people to like you, to understand you, or to want you in their lives. The right people are out there; don't settle for less.

Remember, **you don't have to spend your energy convincing other people of your value. The right people already know.**

STILLNESS VERSUS STAGNATION

Dear friend,

Have you ever felt stagnant—like you weren't making any progress? Ugh, I have. It's the worst. In a major transitional period of my life, I felt overwhelmed with frustration. I was doing everything to move forward, yet life felt so *still*. Were my efforts fruitless? Was anything changing?

The stagnation I perceived was inviting me to dive deeper into my relationship with myself. I wasn't actually stuck, but in a chapter of purposeful stillness, a calm before a storm. It's easy to bypass the in-between moments of life, eager to hop to the next big thing, but in doing so, we miss out on the power of stillness. In stillness, we are presented with truth. When we are still, we can tune in to inner wisdom and guidance that are so often overlooked. It helps to look at it this way: Think of a closed glass jar filled with sand, rocks, pebbles, and water. When vigorously shaken, the elements combine, making the water unclear and murky. Once settled, you can see the different layers within as well as the clarity of the calm water. This is the power of stillness.

Trust your own discernment to know when your life is calling for intentional stillness or a nudge for action.

Remember, in a season of stillness, your truth becomes clear, and your priorities rise to the surface.

WHAT YOUR BEST MEANS

Dear friend,

We all hold ourselves to high standards, but none of us is superhuman. We simply won't have the time, energy, or resources to do it all and do it all flawlessly. And really, that's okay. All you can do is your best with the time and energy you have right now—not at some imaginary time when you're at peak performance.

Today, can you be confident that it's enough to do your best? Can you trust yourself enough to know that your efforts from moment to moment are sufficient, and you don't have to be so hard on yourself?

Your best is always changing from day to day and circumstance to circumstance, so create space and acceptance for the you who shows up today. Maybe you have more to give than yesterday, or maybe you're finding that you need to take a step back. Only *you* know what today's best will be; your core responsibility is to tune in to yourself and honor whatever capacity you have.

Trust that consistently doing your best and staying present will ultimately lead to the success and satisfaction you long for. Give yourself grace in the gaps and be proud of your best.

Remember, doing your best doesn't mean being perfect; it means being confidently, authentically you. You are always enough.

TRUST THE PROCESS

Dear friend,

I don't know about you, but I tend to subconsciously seek control over every little thing that happens to me. And as you can tell by now, trust hasn't always been easy for me. I've allowed difficult situations and disappointments to etch away at my belief that things can go right, and consequently, I tried to regulate all that life could bring. But this quest for control was ultimately futile.

I've learned, instead, to trust the process. The more I can believe that my path won't fail me, the more I can breathe easily and surrender to the natural flow of life.

Trusting the process means challenging overthinking, mindless ruminating, and anxious wondering about when or whether things will happen. It's helpful to stop obsessing about what has gone wrong and cultivate optimism for what will go right. We do not need to micromanage how things unfold; we just have to show up and take action.

Today, try surrendering to the timing of your life—not forcing anything, but leaning back with faith that everything you desire is on its way.

Remember, **you can lean in to the magic and cadence of your own life's timing. Delight is found in the unfolding.**

POSITIVITY SPIRAL

Dear friend,

Have you ever noticed how easy it is for our minds to latch on to negative thoughts? One pops up, then another, and another—next thing we know, our minds have spiraled into a full session of doom and gloom. Negative, unproductive thoughts feel so much easier for our minds to engage with than positive, happy ones. We know the power of our thoughts and how, unchecked, they can wreak havoc on our mental health and emotional well-being.

Here's an antidote to consider: A positive thought and a negative thought cannot exist in the mind at the same time.

As you become more aware of your thoughts, you can better catch yourself when your mind starts slipping into negative, unproductive ones. When you are able to stop it at inception, you can consciously choose a more soothing, nourishing replacement. Think of the positive change you could experience in your life, making this practice a daily commitment. Thought by thought, you can shape how you experience your life. You can start today!

Remember, **you cannot quiet your thoughts, but you can choose which thoughts to engage and which to release. Create a positivity spiral in your mind.**

SHOW UP FOR OTHERS

Dear friend,

I hope there has been at least one time in your life when someone has been there for you in a caring, meaningful way. The kind of support that leaves positive ripples in your life's path. How did that kind of love and care feel? What did it mean to you to truly know you are cared for?

The only better feeling than feeling supported is to reciprocate that love in return. Mutual respect and care are the signs of a truly rewarding relationship. Life feels brighter and more purposeful when we can share it with others.

Today, let's show up for the ones who matter most to us. Is there something you can do to show how much you care? Is there someone who needs to know how much they mean to you? Is there someone who needs support in a season of despair?

When we show up for others, the world feels a little less lonely and isolated; there's no better feeling than this kind of kindness and care.

Remember, **relationships are a two-way street. When you lovingly show up for others, you become an example of how you wish to be loved in return.**

YOUR PATH WILL NOT BETRAY YOU

Dear friend,

How would you feel if I told you that you can't mess up your life? Let me explain. Of course, you'll make mistakes and choose incorrectly, but those actions can't ruin the magnificence of who you are. Does this bring you a sense of peace?

Know that it's common to live in constant comparison, wishing away parts of our lives and longing for what others have. But living for the lives of others rather than embracing our own only leaves us feeling dejected and disheartened.

Today, can you seek to love the path of your own life, knowing it's valid and enough? Your unique path is to be treasured, not belittled. Take heart knowing that what is meant for you in this world will never pass you by. Living in this freedom can be an incredible relief. You might not know the timing of how things will unfold, but trust that your life path will not betray your desires. Today, you will only move closer to them.

Remember, **what is for you won't miss you. Trust the timing of your life.**

YOU CAN TRUST YOURSELF

Dear friend,

Have you ever felt you couldn't trust yourself? I have, and it's truly terrible. During a time when I engaged in a lot of unhealthy behaviors and habits, I found it impossible to trust myself, my judgment, or my instincts. This is an excruciating way to live. Interestingly enough, learning to trust myself was a much harder task than learning to trust others.

Building self-trust is a daily practice. It requires identifying the aspects of your life that aren't serving you and committing to the discipline of change. It means leaning in to your desires and honoring your intuition. Self-trust grows gradually, day by day. You'll feel a deeper sense of inner peace, knowing you won't let yourself down, and you'll learn to respect your own instincts rather than looking to others for direction.

For me, self-trust has opened a new level of self-love, because I can fully own and accept myself in a way never possible before. You deserve to feel that love and trust for yourself. You deserve to feel that freedom and ease. It is never too late to develop a deep relationship with yourself, grounded in love and trust.

―――――――

Remember, **be sensitive to your desires, intuition, and self-confidence, and build trust from within.**

TIME FOR WHAT YOU WANT

Dear friend,

Do you ever feel frustrated that you just don't have enough time for what you really want? That life is filled with what we have to do, leaving no time for what we *want* to do? I've often felt this way, overwhelmed with overcommitment, leaving little room for desired additions.

But with love and respect, as your friend, let me ask: Can you use your frustration as a sign to reexamine your priorities? Can you push back on the belief that there isn't enough time and instead question how you're spending the time you have? Can you expand time for what really matters to you?

When you want something enough, you will always find a way. Today, reclaim your relationship with time and remember your power of choice. If there's something you wish to create in your life, give yourself permission to make it a priority.

———

Remember, **power lives in your ability to choose; spend your energy and attention with presence and care.**

RELEASE UNHEALTHY HABITS

Dear friend,

  I was in high school when my mom first cautioned me about addiction. After my first night overindulging, I learned of my family history of alcohol dependence.

  Despite this warning, I developed a toxic relationship with alcohol. I was in denial for a while, brushing off my patterns as typical young-adult behavior, but I eventually hit my personal rock bottom. I was forced to be brutally honest with myself, no longer making excuses. I couldn't live the life I truly desired if alcohol played a role in it. I had to make the uncomfortable choice to disengage from my toxic patterns, but I was afraid of what that would look like and wondered, *Can I still be social? Have friends? Have fun? Will I be judged or looked down on?*

  I'm so proud of the choice I made to break free from my personal dysfunction. I now can trust and rely on myself, and it's freeing to be able to do so.

  I hope you know there is no shame in admitting you need to make a change. We all have our battles, and it is brave to show up to life facing them head-on. Break free from the patterns and habits that no longer serve you. You deserve this freedom.

Remember, **releasing unhealthy habits takes bravery and strength. You've got this.**

NOTICE SELF-SABOTAGE

Dear friend,

I did everything right! Why did it go so wrong? If you've ever said this to yourself, I am right there with you. It's incredibly disheartening to put in the work, only to feel like your efforts were in vain.

I remember a particularly frustrating time when I was working hard for an outcome, but the results just weren't there. It was maddening, to say the least. Some reflection and brutal honesty with myself unveiled the hard truth that while I thought I was doing things right, I was actually sabotaging my own happiness.

Self-sabotage is common, especially when we are seeking big dreams. Often, we self-sabotage as a subconscious act of self-preservation—a way to stay safe. We hold back from fully putting ourselves out there, hoping to shield ourselves from the sting of rejection. Does this ring true for you?

If you're feeling frustrated with the pace of your life, ask yourself whether there are hidden ways you might be self-sabotaging. This can look like being unclear with your words or actions, procrastinating or avoiding simple tasks, doubting yourself and your abilities, or minimizing your goals and dreams.

Today, keep an eye out for ways you might be holding yourself back and let yourself be free from them.

Remember, **you deserve to live your life fully and completely; release subconscious self-sabotage and watch your life soar.**

PERMISSION TO SAY NO

Dear friend,

For many of us, saying no feels impossible. It's often ingrained in us from an early age to be appeasing, amenable, and always willing to go the extra mile. In theory, these are positive qualities, but for many this has translated into a lack of boundaries and the belief that we do not have the option to decline. This ultimately leads to feeling overextended, overtired, and overwhelmed.

The thing about perpetually saying yes when you want to say no is that, eventually, you get sick of it. You start resenting people, feeling like you have no time for yourself.

I want to remind you of the truth that it's okay to say no. In fact, you're allowed to say no without explanation. You don't have to give a reason for the decisions you make that honor yourself, your safety, your well-being, and your ideals.

Making steadfast decisions that honor your best interests is one of the highest acts of self-care. You're allowed to say no to the people, places, and circumstances that do not serve you and that aren't aligned with who you are and what you want.

Remember, release yourself from the need to please and from the impulse to say yes without discernment. You have a right to say no.

YOU CAN CHANGE YOUR MIND

Dear friend,

Many of us take pride in making wise choices and keeping our promises. We feel good when we're strong in our convictions, knowing that wishy-washiness can be an off-putting trait. So what do you do when you need to change your mind? Do you ever give yourself this option?

For a long time, I rarely let myself change my stance, despite the suffering or agony I was facing. I put so much effort into my decisions that I felt I had to stick with them—no matter what. It didn't matter that I was miserable. My life felt like a tug-of-war—but one I could never win.

Can you relate? Why do we do this to ourselves?

Today, know that you're allowed to change your mind, at any time. Life is fluid, ever-changing, and always showing you new perspectives and information. It makes sense that you're going to change with it. You can change your tune when your heart shifts its desires. You are never stuck.

Remember, it's never too late to change your mind, choose differently, or move in a new direction.

MAKE THE ORDINARY EXTRAORDINARY

Dear friend,

Do you ever find yourself living for the weekend? Do you wish away the ordinary days just to get to a prized day off? It's natural to yearn for good things to come, but rather than waiting for the future, what if you invited some of that weekend peace and levity into your everyday life?

I'm on a mission to make your ordinary life feel more extraordinary. Will you join in? I know how easy it is to become disillusioned with monotony, or maybe even bored with life. But today is what we make of it! It's on us to do our best to be proud of our lives and own exactly who we are, even if we aren't yet where we want to be.

Today, where can you invite the extraordinary into your ordinary? How can you commit to embodying gratitude for every part of your routine and invite a spirit of curiosity and whimsy into your everyday life? Stay present to life and see what comes up from moment to moment.

Remember, **the small moments of your life are just as important as the big ones. Honor and cherish your everyday existence.**

REDIRECTING ANXIETY

Dear friend,

Anxiety often feels ever present and inescapable. Doesn't it seem like everyone always feels anxious? Is there anything we can do about it, or are we just destined to be riddled with angst and dread?

How you manage anxiety is personal; there is no one-size-fits-all method to mental health and emotional wellness. But for me, remembering this truth has helped me talk back to my anxious thoughts: When I feel anxious, it's a sign that my mind has left the present moment.

Anxiety causes us to ruminate about the past or worry about the future, robbing us of the power we have right now. But if we commit to living in the present moment, grounded in reality, anxiety loses its power. Through positive affirmation and reinforcement, we can fight back against these thoughts.

When filled with worry or doubt, double down on your inner strength. If you're feeling afraid or confused, affirm that all is well in this moment. It is comforting to know that you don't have to allow your nagging thoughts to take over; rather, you can remind yourself of your power to redirect and choose again.

Remember, **anxiety would have you believe so many lies about your life, but you have the power to remind yourself of what's true.**

A HARD TRUTH

Dear friend,

By now you know I am a recovering people-pleaser. Much of my young life was spent in desperate attempts to be liked and accepted. It's uncomfortable to admit, but we're all friends here.

So here's the truth: At one point, I believed I could make every person like me. Yes, you read that correctly—*every single person*. This was the depth of my delusion.

As I got older, I started to realize how challenging this wild goal of mine was. Whenever I would experience confrontations and unpleasantries in my relationships, I tried to earn others' affection by making myself smaller, careful not to be "too difficult" or "too much." It didn't work, and I felt so confused. But that's when I *finally* learned this hard but powerful truth: I can't be everything to everyone. I can't force everyone to like me. That is not my job, and it is not my responsibility. I can let that impossible task go.

I found freedom from knowing that I can be okay with not being liked, not being understood, and being judged. You can too. Today, know that you don't actually need every single person to like you, so long as you like yourself.

Remember, **by simply doing what's true and loving for you, you're always doing enough.**

IT'S OKAY TO FEEL LOST

Dear friend,

We've talked about this throughout the year, so we know the importance of knowing and claiming what we want. But today, I'm going to challenge this a little bit, because, as we know, life isn't black-and-white. What if there is purpose and meaning to be found in the *not* knowing too?

It's our nature to crave answers and assurance that we are on the right track. So when we're not sure what we want next, it can be scary and unsettling. But can you give yourself permission to wander during periods of uncertainty?

The roads of our lives will have twists and turns we won't be able to predict. Feeling lost on the path doesn't mean you've failed; it's simply an opportunity to explore new directions.

There is no guidebook to charting your unique path; no one knows how to be you. When you feel lost, accept it as an invitation to dive deeper into your connection with yourself, fortifying the strong foundation you are building within. Let this foundation be your compass, and stay open to what lies ahead.

Remember, **your path is your own. Embrace your life, even its moments of uncertainty, with curiosity and excitement. You can't mess it up.**

FOLLOW THE BREADCRUMBS

Dear friend,

When you find yourself at a crossroads and have a hard decision to make, it's tempting to endlessly agonize over your choices. We often think we need to know how everything might turn out before making our next move. We attempt to play the role of fortune teller, fruitlessly trying to predict the future.

During one time of unbearable uncertainty, a conversation with a life coach changed everything for me. I was encouraged to release the need to know all the answers to my life's questions and instead take notice of the small parts of life that excited me—the "breadcrumbs" on my path. Rather than imagining my five-year plan, I could follow the breadcrumbs in front of me and let them guide me.

If you see something intriguing and feel drawn toward it, go after it. All your little breadcrumbs of happiness add up to a rich and meaningful life. As you follow your breadcrumbs, let go of the worry about where they will ultimately lead. Let your curiosity guide you, and invite excitement for what's to come.

Remember, you will find your path when you follow the tiny joys in life.

FEEL YOUR FEELINGS

Dear friend,

When someone asks, "How are you today?" do you respond with a routine "Fine, thanks," or do you stop to consider what is true for you in that moment?

Perhaps out of self-preservation, autopilot, or fear of what might come up, we tend to bypass these little invitations to check in on our emotions and connect with our feelings. But much valuable insight can be found just beneath the surface. Our emotions serve as a temperature check—a signifier—for what is actually going on in our lives. When we push them down, we disconnect and rob ourselves of the wisdom our feelings can give us.

Maybe you've been told at some point that your feelings make you weak, but the truth is, when you unearth them, listen to them, and work with them, you will inevitably become stronger and wiser—a truer version of yourself. And who doesn't want that?

Today, let yourself connect with your feelings and tune in to that truer version of you.

Remember, **you don't have to fear your feelings. Be open to and curious about what your feelings are trying to tell you.**

OCTOBER 3

BREAK FREE FROM CODEPENDENCY

Dear friend,

Relationships haven't always been my strong suit, and learning how to build healthy relationships has been my biggest teacher. In doing so, I've had to untangle the tricky dynamic of codependency.

It took me a while to identify my codependent tendencies; I was in denial. But when I finally looked in the mirror to face my patterns, it was unavoidable. I lived for approval, attached my identity to others, and diminished my own needs. I was insecure and afraid of being alone, and I thought this was the way to get people to stay. But it was actually the way to codependency, enmeshment, and self-doubt.

Engaging in codependency robs the people in your life of who you really are. It robs the world of your gifts and your magic, because you are masking them to keep the peace. Ultimately, codependency is a no-win game; no one, mainly yourself, benefits from you not living your life true to you.

If you find yourself changing who you are and what you value most to fit in, know you can break the cycle. You don't have to edit your magic to feel loved or cherished.

Remember, **you are worthy of relationships that make you feel safe to be you.**

HONORING GRIEF

Dear friend,

As much as we'd all like to avoid it somehow, grief is simply part of the human experience—and one of the hardest parts. We all have an expiration date, and most of us can never know when our time will come.

Even though we know this to be true, it doesn't take away from the visceral pain, shock, and heartbreak that come when someone we love is taken from us.

When my dad passed away in his sleep, I was heading into my senior year of college, a time that was meant to be happy and carefree. This unforeseen plot twist changed absolutely everything for me. There is the before, and there is the after.

Over time, I've learned to embrace my grief and transform my feelings from sadness and anger to love and remembrance. I've learned that just because a loved one is no longer with us physically, that doesn't mean we can't sustain a loving, personal relationship with them.

Know that grief is a reminder that love was present, and even though it's no longer in its original form, that love still exists. Today, honor the love that you share.

Remember, **you get to decide what kind of relationship you will have with grief. How you grieve is completely up to you.**

LIVE WITH INTEGRITY

Dear friend,

    The numerous, small choices you make each day influence your evolution. Where you go, what you do, how you spend your energy, who you spend your time with—all of these decisions mold and shape you. Choice is where you find empowerment in a world that often feels overwhelming and confusing.

    What happens, though, when you make a poor choice? How can you come back to your strong inner foundation when it feels like you're drifting away from who you want to be?

    For me, the answer lies in returning to integrity. Living with integrity is honoring your soul's deepest desires and values and committing to making choices that align with them. It means recognizing when you are choosing against your own best interests and suffering because of it. Self-sabotage creeps in when you consistently live outside of what you value.

    Take back your power of choice by coming home to yourself and your personal standards. Examine your behaviors and look for opportunities to realign your choices with your desires and dreams. Incredible freedom and ease are found when you live with this kind of authenticity.

Remember, **every day is an opportunity to honor yourself through your actions and choices.**

MOVING ON FROM REGRET

Dear friend,

No one wants to live a life consumed with regret. We can't go back and change the past, nor can we relive old experiences. So how can we learn to acknowledge what happened and let it fuel us rather than deplete us?

You can honor what you wish to change about your past by transforming how you act in the present. Trust that the conscious choices you will make today will show your growth, wisdom, and understanding. In this way, your hardships can become building blocks to create the person you want to be right now.

Can you break free from the shame you carry about your past, and can you seek acceptance today? Release yourself from regret and remorse. Set yourself free from thinking things could have been different, knowing that the only place where you have control and power is the current moment. And the only action that matters is what you do right now.

Remember, **you have so much power in this world, but it is available only in the present moment. Release yourself from regret so you can access it.**

PLAY THE LONG GAME

Dear friend,

Self-discovery has taught me so much and changed my perspective. I've strengthened my connection within and uncovered the inner workings of my mind. But, despite my practices and well-intentions, the nagging mind games that plague me creep in from time to time. Those pesky games? Comparison and self-doubt.

If I'm not careful, when my insecurities are heightened, I tend to default to comparing myself to others, measuring my success against everyone else's. And then, without fail, that small whisper of self-doubt takes hold, causing me to question my abilities and worth. Often these mind games have become barriers to my joy.

With experience, I've gotten better at identifying the start of these games, and rather than allowing them to throw me for a loop, I nip them in the bud.

Your mind games are likely different from mine. With increased attention, care, and introspection, I know you'll make progress in combating the unhealthy games of your mind. The long game of healing consists of practice and persistence. You've got this.

Remember, you can release the habits, mind games, and unhealthy patterns that hold you back. You are making progress.

DON'T FEAR CONFRONTATION

Dear friend,

You may be like me and deeply dislike confrontation. I tend to avoid it whenever I can! But as we know, moments of tension are inescapable parts of life.

While I'm still learning to lean in and approach conflict with peace and confidence, one particular mental reframe has helped me immensely: We're all going to view things differently, experience things differently, interpret things differently, and feel things differently. Knowing this to be true, it's completely natural for our memories of a particular event not to add up, for our wires to cross, and for misunderstandings to take place. With so much variation among us, how could it not?

Embracing this truth helps me remember that I don't have to take confrontation personally. Disagreeing with others does not reflect poorly on my character. It does not make me a bad person. Conflict is simply the natural, inevitable result of unique people doing life together, and healthy conflict resolution starts with recognizing that every person views life through their own lens. We aren't all going to see life in the same way, and that's okay!

Remember, **confrontation happens; rather than avoid it, trust that you can confidently handle anything that comes your way.**

IT'S OKAY TO BE MISUNDERSTOOD

Dear friend,

I was a shy child, quiet and reserved. I hadn't built up my self-confidence, so I often stayed behind the scenes and kept a low profile. My behavior had no correlation to others, and yet many took it personally or held judgment. My quiet nature was often misunderstood.

Have you ever felt misunderstood or not fully seen? It's a frustrating feeling and challenging to process, but we will likely experience it at some point in our lives. We will naturally come up against situations where people do not get us or who we are, and it can feel incredibly isolating. How will you protect your peace when you feel misunderstood or disconnected from someone you love?

Remember, you can't control what happens to you, but you can manage your reactions to it. When you feel hurt or misunderstood, look inward for your validation. That's where true strength and clarity lie. So long as you love and honor who you are, you no longer need approval from other people. Finding the ones who do see and understand you is just a bonus.

Today, release yourself from the internal pressure of needing to feel understood and seeking this aspect of external validation. Isn't it a relief to let this go?

Remember, **it's okay to be misunderstood; own who you are always.**

BE A FORCE FOR GOOD

Dear friend,

You are living in this world at this moment for a reason. You have unique skills, traits, and circumstances that infuse your story with purpose and meaning. No matter where you are or what you are going through, your unique personality adds something beautiful to this world.

Be reminded of the influence and power you have, and let that fill you with confidence, knowing that what you think, do, and say matters. Think about the mark you wish to leave on the world. Contemplate the energy you wish to embody. What will your legacy be?

We are all born with certain privileges and benefits in life, so reflect on what you can do with yours to help others. How might you use your power for good? How will you participate in your day today with a renewed sense of purpose and passion? Never forget that you are a wonder, full of meaning and magic.

———

Remember, **your life has an impact. Every day is an opportunity to engage all of your beautiful, unique qualities, making the world around you a brighter, better place.**

OCTOBER 11

NO MAGICAL ELIXIR

Dear friend,

In a time of extreme personal confusion, I was desperate to find the magical elixir of habits that would "fix" my life. I learned from every teacher I could find, cherry-picking their tips and tricks to make them my own. If it worked for them, surely it would work for me.

In theory, this isn't totally off base; there is a common thread of universally healthy habits. Where I went wrong was in seeking to replicate someone else's life rather than tuning in to my own. I learned from that exhausting cycle that there is no one "right" way to live. What works for someone else, or is another person's magical cure, might not work for me. And that is completely okay.

The beauty of this truth is that you get to design a lifestyle that works for you, nourishes you, and fills your own cup. Take note of the habits you practice daily and how they make you feel. Be curious about what you need at this moment, and give yourself permission to make changes when you need to.

Remember, there is no one-size-fits-all approach to well-being, but when you honor and care for yourself every day, you cultivate an unshakable foundation within.

HEALING AND THRIVING

Dear friend,

I know that because you're reading this book, you're likely someone who desires to be the best version of yourself. You care about yourself and your life, and I'm so happy you do. I'm grateful that you're here!

Still, sometimes we can get so engulfed in personal development and healing that we start to believe we must reach a certain personal destination to be worthy of the life we desire, as if we aren't enough already—right here, right now.

I have found myself believing that if I identify enough toxic habits, release enough unproductive thought patterns, and work through enough past traumas, I'll finally *be* enough for the relationships, jobs, and life experiences I've always wanted. But when I think this way—that I'm not good enough *yet*—I deny myself the good life I could have in the moment.

The truth is, being on a healing path is worthwhile and a valuable use of our time and energy, but that doesn't mean we can't also be happy, productive, and thriving along the way. You were born into this world being worthy and enough. How could your perspective change if you took some time to remember this today?

Remember, no matter where you are on your healing and personal-development journey, you're already enough. You're *always* enough.

NOT WHERE YOU WANT TO BE

Dear friend,

You work so hard to reach your goals and create the life you dream of, and you deserve the life you seek. But in the moments when life isn't progressing at your preferred speed or doesn't quite seem like it's moving in the direction you want it to go, remind yourself of this: You're just not there *yet*.

Can you become open to the belief that your efforts are never unnoticed, that your work is not in vain, and that inertia is moving you forward—even if you can't feel it? Trust that every passing moment moves you closer to what you desire; remember that change is always constant.

So don't give up hope. When your present reality doesn't seem to match up with your future goals, try not to feel down. If you become frustrated or anxious, ground yourself in trust, confidence, and patience. Double down on your convictions and belief in yourself, knowing that your path won't betray you. Stay the course.

Remember, **each chapter of your life has value and purpose. Celebrate what you've lived through up to this moment.**

CHOOSE YOUR BATTLES

Dear friend,

People will push your buttons and you'll encounter conflicts that will spark the need to fight back and defend yourself. Yet so much anxiety and overwhelm stem from never knowing when the next battle will come, causing us to reside in fight-or-flight mode. It's exhausting and draining; you deserve a break.

Can I tell you something today that I hope will put you at ease? You don't have to show up to every battle you're invited to. Does that give you any relief?

This doesn't mean people are going to stop pushing back on you and life is going to be conflict-free. But when and how and whether you engage in the battles that life brings your way remains your choice and your power.

Know this: You can skip the fight. You don't have to argue. You can protect your peace. If engaging in the battle does not align with your current values or ideals or future goals, you're allowed to use your discernment and say no. You don't always have to be in a battle or a struggle. Know where your energy is needed and where you can pull back.

Remember, **you can protect your peace by choosing your battles.**

OCTOBER 15

LIVE FOR YOU

Dear friend,

Do you ever find yourself making decisions strictly to appease someone else? When we are bogged down in uncertainty or doubt, it's easy to give away our power, letting other people decide how we will live. I've been there.

If this resonates with you, know that today can be the day you decide to start living for you. Give yourself permission to listen to the voice within, and allow yourself to feel confident in the choices you're making because you know what's right for you. In standing up for yourself and your desires in this way, you'll start to create a deeper, more meaningful sense of self-confidence and begin to build a life that you can be proud of.

Owning who you are and what you want in this world signifies that you trust yourself and your life path. And living with this self-assurance opens you to so many more people, places, and opportunities that are right for you. It's a win-win.

Remember, **you're allowed to feel confident in your decisions. You're allowed to speak up for yourself and your desires.**

ACCEPT LIFE'S ROADBLOCKS

Dear friend,

If a genie magically appeared before you now, granting you one wish, would you ask for life to be a little easier? For things not to be so hard?

I often think this way. But we can't magically erase our struggles, and we can't avoid life's roadblocks. The way we identify and react to them is what matters most.

Rarely are we given straight paths to our intended destinations; we're typically met with curves, detours, and unexpected delays. How do we handle these aspects of the journey? Do we let them rattle us and question our path? Do we convince ourselves to turn around and abandon it altogether? Or do we approach roadblocks with curiosity, patience, and acceptance?

Remember that any journey toward something meaningful and worthwhile will have unexpected complications. Instead of seeking the perfect or fastest route, fortify yourself by knowing you can handle what comes your way. The roadblocks you encounter in life do not indicate that you are unworthy of your journey; rather, they're opportunities to face a challenge and learn something. Seek to appreciate the road you're on for what it is and where it's taking you.

Remember, **what your unique life has in store for you will always make the journey worthwhile and help you find beauty along the way.**

WHEN IS IT TIME TO LET GO?

Dear friend,

One of the trickiest dynamics in life is knowing when to hold on and when to let go. Whether it's letting go of people or situations, we so often latch on with a white-knuckled grip. Sometimes we're afraid of the unknown, of what will happen if we let go. We might wonder, *How will I fill the void?*

The key is to build trust—both in yourself and in your life in general. When you cultivate the confidence to trust yourself and your discernment, you can release the people, places, and things that no longer serve you. Closing the door on things you once loved isn't easy, and sometimes it may feel like you're going against your best interests. But the truth is, you probably already know if it's time to move on. Pay attention to those subtle inner shifts, listen to your intuition, and take inventory of how you feel around certain people or places. You hold the wisdom to know when it's time to close a chapter.

Today, trust yourself and your instincts. It's safe to let go when you're called to. We have seasons in life for a reason. Trust that you will know when one has ended, and have faith that life will always present you with something new.

Remember, **there is no shame in moving on from parts of your life that no longer serve your best interests.**

YOU KNOW WHAT TO DO

Dear friend,

For a long time, the phrase *I don't know* was a common refrain in my life. This was incredibly frustrating to my mom; she didn't want me to live in denial of my truth. So one day, in response, she asked, "If you did know, what would you do?"

My mom is quite clever. She knew I needed this nudge to figure out what I wanted, and I hated it; she wasn't going to let me off the hook! By asking me this, she was holding me accountable for my desires and making me do the work—and even though I resented it in the moment, it ultimately was the prompt I needed. This question allowed me to remember that I know more than I think I do; I just have to dig for the answers.

Whenever you find yourself thinking you don't know what you want or don't know what to do, think of my mom, and ask yourself, *If I did know, what would I do?* Be open to whatever responses rise to the surface and come to mind.

The truth is, you do know many of the answers to the questions life presents to you. Take ownership of what you want. You know more than you think you do.

Remember, **you are smart enough, intuitive enough, and capable enough to show up to life and make a decision, no matter what is in front of you.**

OCTOBER 19

THE MEANING OF SUCCESS

Dear friend,

I've often defined success by external validation and praise. I was laser-focused on achieving and cultivating it. I often based my success on how I stacked up in comparison to the people around me. As you can imagine, this way of viewing success ran me ragged and kept me from truly being present to the good in my life.

Forced to redefine what success meant, I found a definition that stemmed more from internal satisfaction than external approval or praise. Success to me now looks like confidence, kindness, trust, and presence. I feel successful when I acknowledge my desires, when my actions are aligned with who I am, and when I'm living with the trust that everything is unfolding as it should. I feel fulfilled when I have gratitude in the present moment and excitement for what the future holds.

What does success look like to you? Does your definition align with what you want to feel and who you want to be? You get to craft your own unique, amazing life. Let yourself be fueled by the way you define success.

Remember, **your life doesn't have to look like anyone else's. How you measure your success is completely up to you.**

DECIPHERING YOUR FEARS

Dear friend,

Everything in this world has meaning if we look for it, even the things we're afraid of. Rather than pushing discomfort away, what can we learn by becoming curious about our fears?

We all deal with fear, and honestly, it makes sense. The world can be unpredictable and chaotic, and that's destabilizing. Today, though, remember the purpose fear can serve and the knowledge it can give you.

Notice the parts of your life where fear has taken control and tap into the feelings surrounding those situations. Why are you feeling this way? Is it from past trauma or conditioned behavior? Is it because something you love is at risk? Talk to yourself like you would a friend and seek to uncover the root of your fears.

Without judgment, name and acknowledge your fears, being careful to remember that much of life has given you reason to be afraid. But take heart that you're not bound to these fears forever. By sorting and processing them, over time you can release those that no longer serve a purpose in your life.

Your fears don't need to consume or define you. And as you patiently work through them, you can use your fears to grow stronger.

Remember, **courage, strength, and hope are buried below your fears. You have the power to call them up.**

OCTOBER 21

PERMISSION TO TAKE A BREAK

Dear friend,

This fast-paced, ever-connected world can make us feel like we can't slow down or press Pause on our responsibilities. A nagging worry within us says that if we take a break, we will be left behind, replaced, or even forgotten. We propel through life, almost as if we were living on autopilot. The all-gas, no-brakes mentality makes us believe we'll reach our desired destinations faster, but that's simply not true.

Though seemingly counterintuitive, taking breaks is crucial to a successful life plan. When you pause, you experience regeneration and restoration. Your brain and body simply need breaks to think clearly and operate at their best. If you're plowing ahead in exhaustion, it's likely you're not giving your best or living in alignment with who you want to be.

You get one life. You can't keep powering through forever, friend. Give yourself the gift of time, and know that you are allowed to take a break. If rest feels unrealistic to you, take it slow. Aim to do just one thing well, and let everything else go. Trust that in rest and stillness, you are still moving forward.

Remember, **time spent replenishing your soul is never wasted. You are worthy of a pause.**

IT'S NEVER TOO LATE

Dear friend,

According to Bronnie Ware, a hospice nurse, the number one regret of the dying is, "I wish I'd had the courage to live a life true to myself, not the life others expected of me."[1] When I first heard this quote, it shook me to my core and resonated with me deeply. Does it with you?

We all fall into routines and habits, and sometimes we forget to check in to see whether our lives are still in alignment with our dreams and wishes. If this is you—if parts of your life aren't how you'd like them to be—let today be the day you realign your life and prioritize your desires. Let today be the day you give yourself permission to choose differently and start again.

Life is all about the small steps we take every day that move us forward. As you know, our choices reflect our values and desires. Are your actions in alignment with who you are and what you want? Let yourself go for it: Apply for the job, make the phone call, submit your manuscript, or even seek to reconnect with yourself. What actions will you take to bring you closer to you?

Remember, **it's never too late to live on your own terms. Live a life that you're proud of.**

OCTOBER 23

DIFFICULT PEOPLE

Dear friend,

You know the ones: people who push your buttons in line at the grocery store, coworkers who test your limits, and family members who needlessly egg you on. The world is filled with people who agitate us and get under our skin. So how can we keep our cool when interacting with them?

Dealing with difficult people is an exercise in patience, grace, and understanding, because we can never fully know what it's like to live in someone else's shoes. The best practice is to approach challenging people with empathy and acceptance. Know that you don't have to match another person's energy; you get to choose how you show up.

Keep in mind that you don't have anything to prove, and what people say and do are never a reflection of who you are. Today, breathe in relief knowing that the difficult people in your life don't have to take up any more of your precious time and energy.

Remember, we all walk through this world with unique circumstances and challenges; how we show up and engage with others matters most. Choose kindness.

A REMINDER ABOUT RELATIONSHIPS

Dear friend,

If you're like me, a relationship ending makes you wonder, *What's wrong with me?* I always carried the blame when I lost a friend or a partner, and I let those failures chip away at my worthiness for love and friendship.

Can I remind you that you are not a failure just because you've had relationships that ended? A relationship ending doesn't mean it, or you, failed. It simply ran its course. I have to remind myself of this too, and I hope you can own it today as your truth.

None of your past experiences in relationships dictates your worthiness to find the right people in your life right now. People who are supportive of your hopes, dreams, and values. People who will love you for who you are and who you are becoming.

Release the punishment you place on yourself for losing the people in your life who weren't meant to stay. Trust in your ability to attract and call in the right people for you in this new chapter of your life.

Remember, **each relationship you experience has purpose and plays a role. Don't let a relationship's end make you believe you're unlovable.**

WHO GETS A SAY?

Dear friend,

Sometimes it can be healthy to seek the advice and opinions of trusted loved ones or mentors when we're making major life choices. But we can know we've gone too far when we lose our own opinions in the process.

As you can tell by now, much of my life was spent putting too much emphasis on external sources of wisdom. The more I looked outward, the more disconnected I felt from myself. I lost touch with my inner voice. My reliance on others made me feel like I was living someone else's life. Let me clarify: They weren't giving bad advice, but I had allowed others' worldviews to dictate my decisions. I allowed them to override my judgments and instincts because I didn't believe I could know what was right for me.

That's when I finally had enough. I realized that I didn't want to live according to other people. I decided that my own wants, desires, and beliefs were worthy of my attention, that my own wisdom was worth listening to.

Your path, your life, and how you choose to live it are entirely up to you. If you seek advice, remember that other people's opinions have other people's energy. Stay in alignment with what's true for you. You have the final say in your life.

———

Remember, **when you're connected to yourself, you'll never betray who you are.**

THE NOSTALGIA TRAP

Dear friend,

Don't tell them I said this, but I think I've reached the age when I finally understand the yearning and nostalgia for times past that my parents often expressed when I was a kid. My dad was a perfect example of this. He absolutely loved his college years, and I'd sometimes witness him longing for that specific part of his past. He was almost consumed by it, and as a child, I was often annoyed by his nostalgia.

But I'm not immune to revisiting the past or reliving good times. There is some comfort in doing so—I won't deny it. The trick is not to let ourselves be overtaken by this longing, disassociating from the present moment completely.

The nostalgia trap is real, and we can all fall into it easily, which is why a commitment to being present is key. We can catch ourselves in the moment and reinforce that a lot of good is happening now too.

Recommit to your presence and take note of what you're grateful for today while honoring what you love from your past.

Remember, there is beauty in the past but power in the present. Don't forget to live in the now.

OCTOBER 27

A MAGNET FOR GOOD

Dear friend,

It's no secret that the quality of our lives is impacted by the people taking space in them. Who we spend our time with can lift us up or tear us down. The pain of an unhealthy relationship can make us question our worth, leaving us wondering if there's anyone out there who truly wants to be in our corner.

I know how it feels to be forgotten, dismissed, and left out. Our natural reaction to avoid being alone is to tightly hold on to whomever we can. But as we know, settling for the wrong relationships leads only to heartache and disappointment.

No matter who you are, you deserve at least one person who sees you, knows you, and understands you. If you haven't found that person, don't give up. Take time to reflect on your own magnificence and worth, honoring exactly who you are. In doing so, you'll start to magnetize the right people to your life. Believe wholeheartedly that your people are out there, and they're looking for you too.

Remember, **you will draw the right people to you. Keep honoring and embodying your worth.**

AN UNBOTHERED LIFE

Dear friend,

Do you ever feel like a pinball bouncing back and forth in the game of life? Are you trying to take care of everything all at once? Relief comes from noting that not everything deserves an emotional reaction. Not every situation deserves your energy or time.

When you discern what is and isn't for you, you can live an unbothered life. This results in maintaining control of your emotions and in feeling more in charge of your peace. Being less emotionally attached to everything swirling around you frees you to choose where to put your attention.

You are unbothered when you operate from a place of confidence, calm, and patience rather than anxiety or agitation. Living unbothered is trusting that other people's actions and behaviors aren't personal, and being comfortable to ask questions for clarity, rather than making assumptions out of fear.

Try practicing an unbothered lifestyle by knowing yourself, establishing intentional limits around what deserves your attention, and setting boundaries when needed.

Remember, **nothing is more worthwhile than protecting your peace in a world that breeds chaos. Make your emotions a priority in your life to help you stay unbothered.**

TELL YOUR OWN STORY

Dear friend,

If no one ever told you what a "regular" life was "supposed" to look like, how would you envision yours? What would the story of your life say, who would be in it, and how would you want it to play out?

It's easy to feel like we've been handed a story to live, and we're expected to fit ourselves into a narrow set of expectations. This is confusing because we are beautifully unique people with one-of-a-kind lives. Shouldn't we be trying to break the mold?

You can honor the beauty of your life path by taking ownership of the goals you've set for yourself, even if they look different from everyone else's. If your timeline for accomplishing certain benchmarks looks different, or if you shirk certain expectations altogether, that's okay! You get to be creative with your life because no other life on this planet is exactly like yours.

Remember that you are writing your own story. Decide which themes, tones, and messages you want your story to convey. Where do you want to go? Who do you want to be? How do you want to be remembered? Let go of expectations and have fun writing.

Remember, **you can't mess up your life. All you need to do is show up each day with an open mind and an open heart.**

REMEMBER TO BREATHE

Dear friend,

Do you ever stop to think about how beneficial your breath is? Sometimes we take this magical force for granted. Yet our breathing provides so much more than nourishment and air that keep us alive.

Often, we don't pay much attention to our breath, or even worse, in stressful situations, we don't realize we're barely breathing at all. Have you ever noticed that in those tense moments, you're holding your breath, preparing for the worst to come?

Focusing on your breath can help you relieve your stress, calm your nerves, and tap into your intuition. Your breath is a tool available to you at any time to help ground you in your body and change your mindset in tough situations.

When life feels challenging and you're unsure what to do, take a moment to come back to your breath. Close your eyes and connect with yourself. Notice the simple inhale and exhale of your natural breathing. Do this for however long you need. Find calm and strength in this practice, and let it fortify you from the inside out.

Remember, **your breath is a tool to access the strength you already have within you.**

OCTOBER 31

WHEN YOU DON'T KNOW WHY

Dear friend,

I've had a handful of relationships end by ghosting. When this happens, devoid of information, my mind attempts to fill in gaps with stories and theories of what could have gone wrong. My pursuit of closure often leads to painful, endless rumination.

Our minds are powerful, and we are infinitely creative. But we don't always put our imaginations to good use. How easy it is for us to write vivid, critical stories about ourselves without knowing all the facts! How tempting to fill the unknown with doom-and-gloom scenarios.

Once we notice negative, unnecessary story-writing taking up *way* too much of our precious mental energy, we can conscientiously release this habit and find more productive ways to use our creative gifts. The truth is, you don't have to know the whole story to find closure and move on. When there's no answer to your *why*s, you can decide to appreciate what you have inside you and focus on what you *do* know. Today, protect your peace and your energy and release that need to fill in the details when things go wrong.

Remember, **you can set your mind on writing your future story instead of filling in the past.**

NOVEMBER 1

TRUST YOUR GUT

Dear friend,

With a few decades of life under my belt, I've realized that the adage "trust your gut" is powerful and rings true. The mind and body are connected, signaling to us where to go and what to do. Are we paying attention to them? When you get a pit in your stomach after a conversation, do you take note and reflect? Can you use your body's natural cues to help guide you through this often-confusing life?

Think of a time when you had a sinking feeling in your stomach. What was your body signaling to you? Maybe you've experienced a tightness in your chest due to too much pressure or stress. Your physical reactions are helpful inputs for you to know yourself on a deeper level. They tell you about your limits, your needs, and your desires. It's like you have another language, unique to you, that you speak with your body.

Will you be open to learning it? The next time you get a gut feeling or intuition hits, explore it. Your body is a trustworthy source of direction.

Remember, **trust your gut and let your physical reactions guide you.**

SIGNS OF EMOTIONAL HEALING

Dear friend,

Growth and healing are cornerstones of our lives. It's a worthy endeavor to unpack our pain and strengthen the relationship we have with ourselves, and, admittedly, it's not always an easy one. We know that healing is not a destination or a result; it's a committed lifestyle of curiosity and care. So how do we know if our efforts are truly serving us, especially when the road is rough?

Look for the subtle shifts in everyday moments, not grand results. Healing is when you can admit fault and receive constructive feedback without taking it personally. Healing is when you take space, avoid knee-jerk reactions, and know that disagreements are okay. If you are setting boundaries, have learned your limits, and are taking responsibility, your healing has empowered you.

Acknowledging signs of emotional healing can offer you the confidence to keep going, so today, celebrate how far you've come. Give yourself credit for your efforts. You've done so much work—you should be proud!

Remember, **how you heal is unique and sacred. Do not rush yourself, and don't forget to acknowledge how far you have come.**

PEOPLE COME, PEOPLE GO

Dear friend,

When I was three years old, my parents divorced. While it was amicable and for the best, I unknowingly picked up some flawed relationship beliefs. For instance, I started to believe goodness equated to lasting relationships. And that if I was good enough, caring enough, and loving enough, I could make any relationship last.

So what happened when relationships in my life came to an end? I fought tooth and nail to make the person stay. I changed myself to avoid the abandonment I was so afraid of.

Only recently have I finally released this belief, knowing it's okay for people to leave. When I sense a rift, I try to learn but not judge. I remind myself that no matter what happens, I am always worthy of love, kindness, and care.

Not all relationships are meant to last. Some are meant only to teach lessons or give experiences so that both of you can grow. There is no limit to love in life, and if a relationship is coming to a close, you don't have to try to hold on and keep it alive. Cherish your relationships, but remember that they evolve.

Remember, **the relationships you want to keep in life are with the people you don't have to force to stay.**

AN UNCOMFORTABLE TRUTH

Dear friend,

If you're a peace-loving soul, you might have spent a lot of your life tiptoeing around people's feelings, walking on eggshells to avoid confrontation, and trying your best to navigate relationships unscathed.

You don't want to cause a scene, and you always want to maintain the peace. Sometimes, if necessary, you edit yourself or make your needs small to ensure everyone else is happy and comfortable.

At times it seems like this kind of life *does* bring peace, but it's fleeting. It's the type that's surface-level and that ultimately leads to inner struggle, confusion, and disconnection from those around you. This is an exhausting way to live, isn't it?

It's not your job to make people feel comfortable at your expense. It's not your duty to cower or hide to maintain a false sense of niceness. You don't have to change yourself or your beliefs to uphold a dysfunctional norm.

Your choices and actions might not make sense to other people, and sometimes they may even make other people uncomfortable. But so long as you aren't harming anyone, remember that you are allowed to make decisions that reflect your own care and self-interest.

Remember, you're allowed to live fully and authentically in your truth. Own who you are.

YOU CAN START OVER

Dear friend,

When things get monotonous and stale and your circumstances are no longer serving you, the hope of turning a new page can be just the thing to break you out of your stagnancy. There's something so hopeful about a fresh start!

No matter where you are in life, you have the choice to begin again and change your course. Sometimes people hold themselves back for a multitude of reasons: age, resources, fear, and ability, to name a few. When you find yourself talking down to your desires, cultivate the practice of talking back, reminding yourself of what's true: It is never too late.

What's stopping you from breathing some fresh air into your life? Can you let go of the restrictions you've placed on yourself and allow yourself to dream of what life could look like if you moved forward with your desires? Consider the small steps you could take toward this life you dream of.

How does it feel for you to imagine in this way? How does it feel for you to know that it's never too late to start again?

Remember, **in every moment you have a choice. Know that today you can choose to begin again.**

BECOME A CYCLE BREAKER

Dear friend,

Each of our family lineages carries unique traits and patterns. With all the good our families bring to our lives, they can also bring dysfunction and difficulty, often passed down from generation to generation.

As someone who has been in therapy most of my life, untangling my family's dysfunction, I've learned about the concept of "cycle breaking," where a person begins to identify toxic patterns and conscientiously decides to replace them with new, healthy ones.[1] Our early caretakers are the first ones to shape our understanding of the world. In these formative years, it's common to adopt unhealthy habits as a way of coping, surviving, and seeking care.

Each of us has our own set of difficulties to work through and heal from. Committing to breaking free from unhealthy family patterns can be hard, but it is a worthy and meaningful venture.

Be proud of yourself as you unearth your own unhealthy patterns and consciously choose something different. You have the power to change your life, and you have the creativity and imagination to create new habits when old ones are no longer serving you.

Remember, **you don't have to perpetuate toxic cycles. You can honor your family without carrying on its dysfunction. Break free and choose your own healthy path.**

NOVEMBER 7

BREAK THROUGH BARRIERS

Dear friend,

Writing this book is one of my biggest dreams come true. I've held the vision of sharing my thoughts and lived experiences with you for many years. Though I've had ideas for these letters for quite a while, I subconsciously blocked myself from this dream by doubting myself and discrediting my abilities. I told myself false stories like *I'm not creative enough* or *People won't care what I have to say*. But you're here reading this note today, so you can see I was able to break through my creative barriers. With conscientious effort and intent, I learned to believe in myself and my dreams.

We are all creative beings; we all have magic to share. Today, be vulnerable and seek out the creative parts of you that you've pushed aside or buried within. Do you have dreams or desires calling to you that you've been too afraid to pursue? Give yourself permission to create without filter or fear; don't hide your gifts from the world. I can't wait to see what you do.

Remember, **your life is your masterpiece, and you are the artist; be open to creating.**

PURPOSE CAN BE FLUID

Dear friend,

Do you ever feel like there are a few lucky ones who are born knowing their lot in life? While others question their path or purpose, these people just know.

I was never that person. I often felt pulled in many directions, and I felt like my lack of clarity about my *why* signaled some sort of major flaw in my life. But as I've grown older and wiser, I've realized that this idea of a singular purpose is a made-up construct.

If you find yourself wanting to explore various paths—a few different careers, new places to call home, or assorted fields of study—you can honor your desires! Your wide array of interests doesn't indicate a flaw in your character. It doesn't make you purposeless; it simply means you're multifaceted.

Let's reframe the relationship you have with purpose, stepping away from pressure and into peace. Purpose can be fluid, transforming with you throughout your life. As you become more aware of who you are, you inch closer to the ideals that light you up and give you a new sense of purpose.

Remember, **your purpose will shift and grow as you do. You have the power to choose what gives your life its value and meaning.**

NOVEMBER 9
WHAT ISN'T YOURS TO CARRY

Dear friend,

I consider myself an empath, which means I am easily affected by the energy around me. While I often love this trait, it can sometimes feel overwhelming.

In a recent rough patch, I was questioning myself and feeling frustrated about absolutely everything. At the same time, some close friends of mine were also struggling. On top of all that, world events were projecting a chaos of their own. I allowed the stress of it to compound within me, taking it all on as if it were my own. I felt compelled to try to fix everything while also trying to fix myself. I let my boundaries down and allowed myself to overextend.

At some point I was reminded of the discernment necessary when you are a caring person in a chaotic world. There's plenty of baggage we can pick up along the way in our lives, but we can find relief when we discern what baggage is ours to carry and what we're free to put down.

You are not solely responsible for all the problems of the world. You do not have to be the fixer in this life. Lean in to what is in your power and control, and show yourself grace in the process.

Remember, **you are allowed to let go of what isn't yours to carry.**

RELEASE RESENTMENT

NOVEMBER 10

Dear friend,

We all know the power of forgiveness and the freedom it can bring. But in practice, it isn't always easy to let go. I've had a handful of traumatic experiences (as I'm sure you have too) that left me clinging to anger, sadness, resentment, and sometimes even a need for revenge. When we feel that we've been wronged, we want it acknowledged, we want to be seen for it, and we want others to know that this is why we are the way we are.

A common response to painful events is to shut off parts of ourselves so we can be protected from future hurt. But in doing so, we also cut ourselves off from our truest selves and our ability to experience life to the fullest.

When I think of freedom in my life, I think of the version of me not consumed by anger or resentment, the one that is unapologetic about who I am. I'm released from the past, knowing that it no longer has an influence on me.

Today, I hope you will set yourself free from the weight of the past. Give yourself permission to feel, forgive, and let go.

Remember, **in being open to releasing resentment, you set yourself free.**

NOVEMBER 11

KNOW WHEN TO MOVE ON

Dear friend,

One of the hardest lessons we can learn is knowing when to stay, when to change, and when it's time to move on. These moments are not easy to discern, and our uncertainty can overwhelm us and paralyze us with fear.

When you're faced with a crossroads and unsure which path to choose, take an inventory of the situation to gain clarity. When you pause, connect, and tune in to your desires, the answers you seek will find you.

Are you sensing a change on the horizon? Be curious and inquisitive. Ask yourself:

> *What do I need in this moment?*
> *What actions can I take?*
> *Am I feeling stuck or inspired?*
> *Where do I need to let go?*

When you connect with your feelings and tap into what you really want, you can uncover the small clues that will guide you in your next steps. Listen to how your inner voice is directing you today.

Remember, **there is no road map for your unique, magical journey, but when you connect with yourself, you can confidently forge your path.**

EMPOWERED DECISIONS

Dear friend,

We are magnetic and attractive to others when we live from a place of authenticity. When you own your desires and speak up for what you want, you're being truthful with yourself and with those around you. But like all new habits and practices, this is something to work on daily. When asked for your preference, don't respond with "I don't know" or "I don't care," because that's not true. In most cases, you *do* know and you *do* care. Will you allow yourself to express your desires? Will you allow your authentic self to be known?

You are dynamic when you approach the world from a position of confidence. And the good news is, confidence is a muscle you can build with every choice you make.

Ask yourself, *What do you want to do? Where do you want to go?* As you encounter questions like these today, view them as opportunities to voice your authenticity and fully own who you are and what you want.

Remember, **your wants and desires are worthy of being voiced. You are allowed to speak up and make choices that fit with who you are and what you want.**

THE ROOT OF YOUR FEELINGS

Dear friend,

I hate feeling stuck—don't you? Sometimes it feels like things will never change and we will be forced to live in our current, stagnant state forever. But don't forget the constant evolution happening in your life and all around you. If you're frustrated with your life's timing, or you feel stuck in a groove that isn't working for you, know that you don't have to live in that feeling for long.

One of the best ways I've found to get out of a long, looming rut is to examine my feelings about the present situation. What is it about my life right now that is making me feel this way? What specifically do I want to change? And why?

Understanding the root of your feelings, especially when you feel stuck, can help you discover actions and steps you can take to move forward. This kind of self-examination can help you make changes that matter—changes that benefit your soul and help you flourish.

Dig deep to understand what you want, and have faith that your life is ever-changing and growing.

Remember, **you are not stuck; you are just in a phase of evolution. Connect with yourself to uncover the steps you're being asked to take.**

RELEASE RELATIONAL PAIN

Dear friend,

Nothing stings quite like a broken heart. I'm sure we can all remember our first heartbreak—how devastating it felt and the fear that washed over us, thinking we would never feel whole again.

The pain of heartbreak often led me to believe I was unlovable, and for far too long, I held tightly to that belief. I saw each broken relationship as a personal failure, a reinforcement that I was broken. I carried my unresolved pain into new relationships and let it cloud my vision in fear.

Heartbreak has taught me the powerful lesson of truly letting go. We don't have to carry the wounds inflicted by our past into our present. Time does heal wounds, and even though we may think our hearts won't mend, eventually they do.

Today, can you lovingly release yourself from the hold of your past? Think of the strength, resilience, and perseverance you have gained after being faced with heartache. Be proud of the progress you have made and of your healing.

Remember, so many people—some you haven't met yet—will love, honor, and cherish you for exactly who you are. Stay open to receive them.

STOP APOLOGIZING

Dear friend,

Can I ask you to consider something that might be a little controversial? I want you to stop apologizing. Before you think I'm nuts, let me explain. I don't mean cutting out apologies altogether but rather taking a deep look into your life and noticing where you are apologizing unnecessarily and asking why.

I used to apologize for everything. It was a defense mechanism and a way I thought I could make people like me. I'd apologize for things that weren't my fault or that were out of my control, and it became a habit.

Friend, taking responsibility for things you're not responsible for is exhausting and confusing. And saying sorry when you're not tends to dilute the power of a true apology.

I've stopped apologizing for changing my mind or forming a new opinion when learning new information. I've stopped apologizing for not living up to other people's expectations. I've stopped apologizing for things I'm passionate about and for what matters most to me. And I no longer feel bad about setting healthy boundaries as a form of self-care.

What will you stop apologizing for today?

Remember, **in discerning what you are and are not responsible for, you cultivate power and inner strength.**

SET MEANINGFUL INTENTIONS

Dear friend,

    I was pretty disconnected and unfocused in my early twenties. I struggled with self-doubt, indecision, and low self-worth, and I didn't really know who I was or what I wanted. I found solace in yoga. It was the first place where I felt the safety and space to really get to know myself. There, I learned to be present and feel at peace within.

    I credit yoga for jump-starting my path and teaching me endless life lessons. It's where I discovered the powerful role that intention can play in our lives. I had never before considered how beneficial it is to be clear with myself before making a move. I had mostly lived in a constant state of reacting to life rather than mindfully engaging with it.

    Being intentional changes everything. It requires you to gain clarity on your true desires, to tap into the truth you carry deep inside. When you know what you want, intention is the vehicle that will take you there. Intention allows you to approach each day with purpose and focus, bringing your daily rhythms into alignment with your truth.

    What intention do you wish to set today? Connect with yourself and listen for the inner whispers of desire.

Remember, **intentions set your dreams into action. Know what you want and be confident in your worthiness of it.**

YOUR LIFE HAS SEASONS

Dear friend,

Just like our environment, your life has seasons too. Each flower blooms at its own pace, vegetables and crops have peak times for growth, and some animals hibernate for preservation. Every living thing has its own set of needs, its own rhythms of productivity and rest.

These are regular parts of the natural world, and we accept these cycles in nature. So why do we resist accepting them for ourselves?

Think about the seasons of your life and observe your unique cycles. What does it take for you to thrive? What do you need to recalibrate? Work, rest, play, and stillness—we need all of these at different times and in varying ways if we want to flourish.

What season are you living in today? Are you in a time of creation? Restoration? Exploration? Contemplation? Now ask yourself, *Are my actions and habits supporting this season of my life?* Don't be afraid to adjust your choices to better accommodate your season.

Remember, be mindful of the seasons of your life. Care for yourself accordingly.

A WORD ABOUT GASLIGHTING

Dear friend,

While we may never fully understand why people behave as they do, we can grow wiser in detecting harmful patterns of behavior. One of the most insidious psychological behaviors is "gaslighting," a practice of misleading and confusing someone so that they doubt their own experience.[2]

If someone is pressuring you to question your abilities or is leading you to believe that everything is always your fault and is never taking responsibility for their own actions, you might be in the presence of a gaslighter. Knowing what to look for can empower you to make choices to protect your mental and physical well-being.

I want you to know that you are not to blame for being gaslit. Remember, this is a form of emotional manipulation and abuse. This is never your fault, and you don't deserve this.

If you're aware that you're being treated this way, set a boundary against the gaslighters in your life. Let today be the day you take back your narrative and reaffirm that you can trust yourself.

Remember, **you are worthy of feeling safe, supported, and understood in your relationships. Mistreatment and abuse are never your fault.**

TUNE IN TO GRATITUDE

Dear friend,

Life is all about perspective. If we look for them, we can always find the bad, upsetting, and disappointing moments, or we can seek the opposite—moments of goodness, kindness, and achievement.

Are you a glass-half-empty or glass-half-full kind of person? If you're easily angered by every little inconvenience or you find yourself saying, "Of course this bad thing is happening to me," it may be that you're living in the glass-half-empty category.

To unlock a glass-half-full mindset, gratitude and presence are the keys. You can cultivate gratitude in even the harshest moments by finding acceptance for life as it is and tuning in to what is going well—these are simple but life-changing shifts that can increase your happiness, even without making changes to your circumstances.

A glass-half-full life is available to those who have cultivated inner strength, to those who trust their own ability to create joy from within. How great is it to live openhearted, tuned in to your own magic!

Remember, **in any moment of life, there is something to be grateful for. Open yourself to the small, magical moments that come from unexpected places.**

ADD FUN TO YOUR LIFE

Dear friend,

When was the last time you really had fun? Do you find it hard to fit fun into your schedule? Simple joys are all around you, if you allow yourself the pause and presence to look for them.

Recall the lighthearted, slow days of childhood, when you had few responsibilities and pressures. What did you do for fun? When did you feel the most carefree and alive? Where did you go to be fully yourself, without any judgment or expectation?

Notice what answers arise when you ask yourself these questions, and track any consistent activities or themes that have stayed with you into adulthood.

For instance, I've recently become a puzzle enthusiast. It feels nostalgic and pure to piece together a masterpiece. And it's totally surprising to me. I never would have considered puzzles to be a source of fun in my adult life, but I'm glad I had the curiosity and openness to try it.

What can you do to bring fun back into your life? I'm so excited for you to find out!

Remember, **there is space in your life for joy. Give yourself permission to do the things that light you up, without any expectation or judgment.**

LEAD WITH AUTHENTICITY

Dear friend,

I think we can agree that honesty is a good quality, in theory. But when you feel under pressure, do you ever find yourself reaching for a white lie? Do you ever hold back your true opinion, tell tiny lies to get out of a tricky situation, or hide parts of your life that embarrass you—all to make someone else more comfortable?

Ultimately, these untruths aren't worth it. The energy it takes to hold back your opinions and push down your emotions is just too much. Your power lies in the simple practice of living truthfully.

Perhaps you fear rejection for speaking your truth, but you may find exactly the opposite. Leading with authenticity and honesty can strengthen your relationships because others can relate to the *real* you. Living openheartedly also gives permission to the people in your life to express their opinions with ease, and they will feel more comfortable opening up to you.

Take stock of the ways you might be muting the seemingly embarrassing or contrarian parts of you, and commit to living more in your truth. You are worthy of experiencing the freedom of honest living.

Remember, **your truth matters, and it's valid. Find freedom in telling the world who you really are.**

NOTICE YOUR SELF-TALK

Dear friend,

You've heard me say that you are the only person who knows what it's like to live your life. You're the only one who knows your experiences, your challenges, your highs and lows. You're the only one who knows what it's like to walk in your shoes and see things the way you do.

You're also the only one who knows how you talk to yourself every single day; you witness how you treat yourself and how—or whether—you love yourself.

I'd like to ask you to examine the script you play in your mind. Are you kind? Loving? Supportive? Do you extend yourself grace and understanding?

So many of us are our own harshest critics. We judge, blame, and pick ourselves apart. We overthink and overanalyze our thoughts and behaviors, and constantly lead ourselves to believe we aren't good enough.

Instead of this, give yourself permission to treat yourself like you would your most cherished friend in this world. Talk to yourself with kindness and compassion. Remind yourself that you are your own best friend, that you are a joy to be around, and that you matter always.

Remember, **you have the power to change how you view and treat yourself. Love, honor, and accept who you are, unapologetically.**

LEARN TO LET GO

Dear friend,

Learning to let go is much easier said than done. Theoretically, we know there's power in a life of surrender—an ease that comes when we go with the flow. But emotionally, it's not that simple.

We like to feel in control, so when faced with ambiguity, or when life takes an unexpected turn, it makes sense that we would fall into old traps of inflexibility. But when we tightly grip our preconceived ideas about how our lives should go, we embody a stale, stubborn energy. None of us want that!

How can you learn to let go and feel good about it? Know that letting go is not an act of complacency or weakness, but a sign of maturity and strength. It means you have built trust with yourself and are confident to stay open to whatever life brings.

Removing yourself from the pressure cooker of perfectionism creates space for new directions and possibilities. Letting go means patiently, faithfully trusting that what you desire will find its way to you. You can hold firmly to what you want while remaining open to all that could be.

It will feel freeing when you do. Give it a try, friend.

———

Remember, **you're allowed to let go and be open to the surprises of life.**

VULNERABILITY IS A BRIDGE

Dear friend,

Years of living in a harsh world full of rejection and ridicule can cause us to close ourselves off from others. We teach ourselves to bottle up our deepest feelings and insecurities for fear of judgment. But we can experience an amazing sense of freedom and connection when we choose to live with our hearts wide open. As risky as it is, embracing a spirit of vulnerability and sharing our souls with like-minded people can unlock the support and community we long for.

A few years ago, I shared online that I had made the decision to stop drinking alcohol. Though I felt fully confident in this choice, I was afraid. I agonized about what people would think of me, whether they would judge me, whether they would write stories in their heads about how I had landed at the decision.

Despite this fear, I shared anyway, and the feedback I received was remarkable: private messages of shared experiences and feelings as well as public encouragement and praise. My vulnerability made me feel strong and connected, both to myself and others.

So today, know that being vulnerable is not a weakness; being vulnerable is one of the strongest things you can do. It is brave to share your life openly, without fear.

Remember, **your vulnerability is a bridge to connection in your life.**

NOVEMBER 25

PROGRESS, NOT PERFECTION

Dear friend,

We all have hard days, but we are stronger than we think. Remember that growth is not linear, so if you find yourself a little more tired, impatient, or unfocused today, take the long view and let it go. Accept today for what it is and commit to coming back to yourself tomorrow.

Let this notion of resiliency fuel you, especially if you feel like you're not quite where you want to be or you're being hard on yourself. Commitment to slow, small progress is the best way forward, so if you're beating yourself up, take the pressure off. Self-forgiveness will always serve you better in the long run.

Hold space for everything you've already been through, knowing it's brought you to where you are now. Breathe in the grace and courage it has taken you to make it this far, and honor yourself for all you have done. Know that each moment of your life is moving you forward; you're not behind.

Every moment is meaningful and purposeful. It can be messy, but that's progress. And your progress is yours to celebrate.

Remember, **the work you do every day is meaningful. Honor yourself for all that you've accomplished on the way to your goals.**

COEXISTING WITH CRUELTY

NOVEMBER 26

Dear friend,

Mean words sting, and it can be disorienting and confusing when we are faced with unnecessary attacks and cruelty. An uncomfortable truth is that we must learn to coexist with people who are unkind to us. We can't change their behavior and we can't change them, but we can reflect and consider how to handle these interactions.

How people behave toward you is not a signifier of who you are. I've found it's true what they say: "Hurt people hurt people." They are living with unresolved trauma and have bottled up their emotions. Most likely, they lack awareness of the impact of their words.

Remember, the poor behavior of someone else has no bearing on who you are. Try not to take unkind behavior and mean-spirited actions personally. Create distance between you and unkind people in your life, knowing it is their responsibility to mend their behavior, not yours.

Remember, **people's behavior says nothing about you. Focus your attention on who you want to be and how you will respond.**

OVERCOMING COMPASSION FATIGUE

Dear friend,

Take a deep breath and be still. I know you have so much on your plate and your time is precious, but notice how being present to this one inhale and exhale brings a welcome feeling of peace.

You care about life deeply, and with endless expectations, you likely desire to do your best always and to never disappoint. Those of us who lead with heightened empathy and compassion can easily overextend if we don't carve out the necessary time to restore our energy. As wild as it may seem, you *can* care too much, leading to compassion fatigue as you become overwhelmed and exhausted by immense feelings.

It's a gift to be so committed to the well-being and happiness of all. We need more people who hold those noble desires. But when we care so fiercely for others, we often lose sight of the limits to what we can withstand emotionally. The adage is true: "You have to fill your own cup before you can seek to fill others'."

So today, I hope you hear this truth: You can be kind and caring *and* say no to protect your peace. Know that you can take space to breathe and connect, restoring your energy. You deserve this care.

Remember, **your kindness and care are gifts to the world; you're allowed to protect your heart.**

PURPOSE, NOT PRESSURE

Dear friend

From a very young age, we are asked what we want to be when we grow up. Our culture puts great emphasis on finding clarity about our purpose, so when we think we don't have it all figured out, we're left feeling directionless and confused. It can be overwhelming to try to home in on what we are meant to do with our one precious life.

If you feel this way, don't be discouraged; you are not alone. We all experience the external (and internal) pressure to find our lives' purpose.

Purpose is an expansive term that can be defined in many ways, so give it a meaning that works *for* you, not against you. Personally, I find purpose in focused presence and intention. Rather than a grand notion of life purpose, I look for the small moments of purpose in my daily life. I am purposeful with my presence and find guidance through it.

How will you define *purpose* in your life? Where can purpose bring you peace and meaning in an aligned way?

———

Remember, **you can define and redefine your purpose at any time. You're meant to be here, and you matter.**

SAVE YOUR ENERGY

Dear friend,

My favorite song of all time is John Mayer's "The Age of Worry,"[3] in which he encourages the listener to persevere and make the most of life despite its challenges. The song encapsulates how I relate to worry. I acknowledge that it's real and choose optimism instead.

What about you? How do you approach worry?

If you feel that worry gets the better of you most of the time, ask yourself, *How can I reframe my worries and happily coexist with them?* The truth is, worrying doesn't solve the problems you have; it just drains your energy and takes you down a mental spiral.

Rather than surrendering your precious mental energy to all the things that could go wrong, give your mind a break and contemplate the things that can go right. Practicing optimism will create fresh grooves in your brain, so you can know that you are strong and capable of moving through life well. Let worry go, friend. You've got this.

Remember, **you can release needless worry and cultivate a sense of trust that your life is unfolding just as it should.**

YOUR MENTAL HEALTH MATTERS

Dear friend,

We've been conditioned to think of health as primarily a physical pursuit, and it's easy to conceptualize wellness as a physical practice because we can see the effects of it more easily. This is why I think it's sometimes hard to prioritize our emotional well-being; it's completely internal, and we can't always see our progress. So we give up on it or push it aside.

I'd like to remind you: Everything you do for yourself is important, and the time you spend caring about your well-being is a wise investment. Taking care of yourself, in every sense of the word, matters. Strengthening your mind and caring for your soul are important. Whatever you need to do today to take care of your mental health, know that it is worth the effort, whether that means taking a few moments in your car before work to breathe, journaling some of your anxious thoughts, or reaching out to a supportive loved one.

You deserve to feel supported and cared for, and you deserve to feel at peace within your body and your mind. Never let anyone question the value of your mental health.

Remember, **taking care of yourself—mind, body, and soul—is a necessary part of your life.**

DECEMBER 1

MOVING THROUGH THE MUD

Dear friend,

I'm a sucker for holidays. Whatever the holiday may be, I'll embrace it and go all in. So imagine my surprise a few years ago, when my favorite holiday season arrived and I felt no happiness at all. I was in a dark place, and no matter how many self-care tools I relied on or therapy sessions I attended, I couldn't lift myself out of the heavy mud in my mind.

This was the happiest time of the year, the season I always looked forward to. How could I not get myself together and find joy? Everything felt like it was too much, to a point where I wanted to give up. This rock-bottom of my mental health was painful, but it ultimately led me to a path of greater fulfillment.

Dark moments are reminders that life isn't perfect, emotions are complicated, and you don't have to fake happiness. You also don't have to go through your struggles alone; there is so much power in seeking support and care. You are not weak for needing help. It's okay not to be okay, and it's okay to be in the mud.

Remember, **a lot of beauty grows out of mud, if you stick around to see it bloom.**

THIS WILL PASS

Dear friend,

Life is filled with traumatic incidents and uncomfortable moments that take us out of the present and make us feel scared, unsafe, and confused. These situations change us, shape us, and leave lasting scars on our souls. No life is lived without heartache and hurt.

Because hardship is inescapable, it's one of the few things that unite us. And often, when bad things happen, there's nothing we could have done to prevent them or prepare for them. It's simply part of life. I hope this truth provides you with a sense of freedom and peace.

Today, if you're feeling overwhelmed by your journey's challenges, know that it's normal to feel nervous, confused, and hurt, and trust that your feelings won't last forever. You should also know that if life has been extra hard on you lately, the difficulties you're experiencing are never an indicator of your worth.

If you are reading this right now, you have made it through 100 percent of your bad days, and that's a pretty good stat to hold on to. Have hope for a brighter tomorrow.

Remember, **no feeling is final. This, too, shall pass, and you are always stronger than you think you are.**

YOU DESERVE PRIVACY

Dear friend,

Have you ever revealed something you wish you had kept to yourself? Overshared to breed connection? You are not alone—not by a long shot.

We live in a world where it's common to share intimate aspects of our lives, both online and in person. We feel pressured to share because we know vulnerability helps people connect with us. And we want to be relatable and trustworthy.

It's true that telling your stories and life experiences can help you connect and feel less alone in life. But equally important is discerning what you tell and when you tell it. You never need to expose personal parts of your life in order to be understood or appreciated—even if someone asks. You have the right to share your story when you feel ready.

If you're feeling pressure to share parts of yourself you're not comfortable sharing, you can be assured that you have the power to keep your life private. You're allowed to hold the tender, sensitive moments for yourself and your trusted few.

Remember, **you don't have to share aspects of your life that you aren't ready for the world to know. Your privacy is important; honor it.**

HONOR EVERY VERSION OF YOU

Dear friend,

Every once in a while, I'll go through old photos, emails, and text messages. I love to feel nostalgic about happy moments in the past and reflect on how far I've come.

Sometimes, though, I've felt that cringe of embarrassment while looking back on past versions of myself. I'll automatically pass judgment on my looks, my personality, and my desires (and even my fashion choices). Shame and criticism flood my thoughts.

In my heart, I know I'd never judge someone else for who they used to be. If I can hold this compassion and understanding for others, why don't I offer it to myself?

Friend, much power comes when you honor and accept the person you once were, knowing that in past moments, you were exactly who you needed to be. Rather than judging and criticizing yourself, what if you embraced who you were, knowing that person brought you to where you are now and will ultimately bring you to where you want to be?

We are not the same people we were one minute ago, one month ago, or one year ago. Let today be the day you stop judging yourself for who you were and start loving each version of you.

Remember, **you're always doing the best you can with what you have been given. Release any shame or judgment you feel for your former self.**

DECEMBER 5

A LIGHT FOR YOUR PATH

Dear friend,

Values signify what matters most to you. So ask yourself, *Do I know what I value, and am I in tune with my values on a regular basis?*

For a chunk of my life, I actually thought I didn't need values. Maybe it was an act of rebellion or defiance, but I believed values were insignificant. I was almost the kind of person who stood for nothing, so fell for anything.

I learned from this confusing chapter that values are important; they root us in what matters most to us. Values illuminate our paths, showing us where to go. In the absence of them, we'll feel pressured to mindlessly adopt the values of the people around us.

What you value is as unique as your own human existence. You don't have to conform to others' values that have been placed on you. Allow yourself to check in with your personal values system. Feel inspired and empowered, knowing that what matters most to you influences every part of your life, if you let it.

Remember, **when you feel lost, tap into your values; they will guide and inspire you on your life's path.**

YOU ARE NOT A BURDEN

DECEMBER 6

Dear friend,

It's possible you've experienced situations that led you to put your needs, wishes, and desires on the back burner. Over time, many of us hold back on voicing what we want, for fear of being "too much."

As strong, confident, independent people, we often think we can handle everything on our own. We tend not to want to bother others with our problems. Not to be a burden, we hold ourselves back and close ourselves off.

If you relate to this, I want you to know that you are never a burden. You're allowed to ask for help, and you're allowed to take up space.

Life is difficult, and you'll often need to rely on others for care and support. This is not "too much." Sometimes asking for help is the most kind, compassionate thing you can do for yourself. Let the loving people in your life be there for you and support you. Affirm to yourself today that you are worthy of love, care, and kindness, and you don't have to go through life alone.

Remember, you are not a burden; your needs matter. Let the people in your life support you when you need it.

DECEMBER 7

NO ONE LIKE YOU

Dear friend,

Here's an exciting truth: You are the only *you* in this entire world. Only you contain your unique combination of gifts, qualities, traits, and abilities. You are quite literally one out of billions! But if you're like me, you know how easy it is to forget this powerful truth and fall into endless comparisons and self-criticism.

Every day we are presented with limitless opportunities to compare ourselves to others, and if we take them, we'll collect all the reasons why we don't measure up. Just think of how much time and energy you spend yearning to be more like someone else or even to be someone else altogether.

What if you used that time and energy to better appreciate who you are? How much happier might you be?

Let's break the comparison cycle and remember the magnificence of your unique self. If you're prone to comparative thinking, focus on the parts of your life that you love. Allow yourself the time to bask in your unique qualities, showing deep love and respect for who you are. In doing so, you encourage others to do the same for themselves.

Remember, no one else in the world is like you. You do not need to compare yourself to others. Who you are is always enough.

STAY HOPEFUL

Dear friend,

During a frustrating chapter of my life, filled with existential dread and confusion, I was desperate for answers or solutions. I can vividly remember sitting in my apartment, wallowing in self-pity, yearning for peace. This desperate moment led me to a silly internet quiz that claimed it would help me find my life's theme song, and I thought that maybe it would give me the answers to my life I was trying so hard to find. (Yes, I know how this sounds.) I answered all the questions, and my theme song populated: "Don't Stop Believin'" by Journey, a classic.

I cried when the results came through, because in that moment, it was exactly what I needed. I needed a reminder that no matter what happens, I didn't have to stop believing in the good or that something exciting can always be on the horizon.

If you're feeling a little desperate today, take hope wherever you can find it! Keep an eye out for tiny joys, silver linings, and little nudges from life that remind you you're on the right track. No matter what is happening in your present experience, curious optimism can maneuver you through the good and not-so-good aspects of life.

Remember, don't let your life or its difficulties keep you from believing in the good. Dare to hope for a better future.

THE WHISPERS OF YOUR HEART

Dear friend,

Do you remember when you were little and you enjoyed life in a pure, unfiltered way? As a child, I loved to dance, but as time passed, I allowed it to fall away from my life. In adulthood, I yearn to reconnect with the dancer I once was. And I'm finding out that it is never too late to listen to those instincts and desires.

What you want in life is divinely inspired. You don't have to feel guilty or unworthy of the things that make you happy or excited. Your desires are the whispers of your heart, and they are begging to be listened to. These internal pulls are made to light you up and point you in the direction of your dreams.

Can you give yourself permission to listen to the voice inside you—the voice of the real you that isn't afraid of judgment or criticism? Let this voice give you the confidence to act accordingly. It doesn't matter what your actions look like from the outside; all that matters is how they make you feel. Tap into your deeply seated wants, take action in alignment with them, and experience your desires coming true.

Remember, **your desires can guide you to the life of your dreams. Listen to what your heart is telling you.**

THE ART OF SURRENDER

Dear friend,

I've never really considered myself to be a controlling, type A person. So imagine my surprise when, during a pivotal chapter of my young-adult life, a mentor of mine encouraged me to lighten up and let go.

I truly believed I was open to life and its possibilities, but in reality, I was pretty closed off. I was chill about the small details of my life but was attempting to control the big picture with a white-knuckled grip.

When I read *The Surrender Experiment* by Michael A. Singer,[1] I was introduced to the notion of living with curiosity and openness, allowing for unexpected guidance. *Surrender* means making plans but being flexible with the outcome. It's releasing the rigidity of how we think our lives should look, with receptivity to something better than we could imagine.

Tune in to yourself and notice the places in your life where you might be closed off to something new. If you find yourself constantly saying no, are there areas in your life where you can say yes?

Remember, **through curiosity you can experience the magic of life. Don't resist your path; surrender to what it could be.**

YOU HAVE PURPOSE

Dear friend,

I believe, without a shred of doubt, that each one of us is here at this time for a reason. I wholeheartedly trust that we all have purpose and that we all matter.

Whether or not you hold a position in a high place, whether or not you're a notable public figure, regardless of where you live and what you do and what you look like, you have impact and meaning. Know that you are powerful in your own right, simply because you are here, alive, in this moment.

When faced with life's existential questions—*What does it all mean? What is my purpose?*—remind yourself just how miraculous it is that we are all here, together, at this time. Each human's unique presence and energy is a piece to a puzzle, each one of us contributing to the beautiful tapestry that is this world.

Today, take in the truth that your presence matters, and notice how it feels to honor yourself this way.

Remember, your presence is important in this world. We wouldn't be the same without you.

MAKE SOMEONE'S DAY

Dear friend,

Have you ever felt so down and dejected that even your toolbox of self-care practices couldn't lift your spirits?

These moments in life when it feels like nothing is working are soul-crushing and overwhelming. I've been there. During a particularly hard time, I reached out to a friend for help. She lovingly encouraged me to step outside of my suffering and, instead, put my energy toward helping someone else.

This was the exact advice I needed, guiding me to shift my perspective. When I went to volunteer for the day, I stepped out of my own life and problems and focused on bringing goodness for someone else. Being present for others allowed me to release the intense feelings I was having for myself. I was filled with relief.

When life feels hard and nothing seems to work, make an effort to make someone else's day. This small shift in attention—turning outward toward another—can renew your spirit and help you cultivate hope and gratitude. Never discount the power of actions done with kindness, care, and love.

Remember, **we are in this life together. Lift your spirits by lifting up someone else.**

BEFRIENDING TIME

Dear friend,

When I was a little girl, I felt like we were always in a hurry and always running late. My mom, whom we lovingly labeled the "Time Demon," often felt like there weren't enough hours in the day. She was juggling many responsibilities with little help, and time felt scarce.

One day, while heading out the door to go to school, I looked at my mom and asked, "Mom, are we going to be in a hurry today?" She credits this as the wake-up call she needed to reevaluate how she was approaching her time management.

When we make rushing a way of life, we take on a frenetic energy and a scarcity mentality that can make us feel scattered and overwhelmed. If that's you, could it be time to reevaluate? What if time were your friend rather than an enemy, a precious resource rather than a scarce commodity?

By slowing down and being mindful, you can expand your sense of time, find peace, and use each moment a little more wisely. It seems counterintuitive that slowing down helps you find more time, but it's true. Be present to each moment as it comes today and let that show you how to make friends with the time you're given.

Remember, **when it feels like time is getting away from you, invite a spirit of presence and slowness.**

WHERE TO FIND INSPIRATION

Dear friend,

We live in a world with endless influence and inspiration, and we get to choose where to take our inspiration from. Have you reviewed the influences in your life and how they make you feel? Try asking yourself these questions:

> *Who inspires me?*
> *Who makes me feel hopeful and optimistic for what's to come?*
> *What people or places move me to be better or do something I've never done?*

Cultivating sources of inspiration has comforted me, empowered me, and shown me a path when I've felt lost. I find motivation in books, workshops, and speeches from people I admire. I'm grateful for the role these people play in my life, even if they don't know it.

Comfort and healing come when we recognize our shared lived experiences. We can relate to people who have similar struggles and find strength in knowing that because they made it, we can too. This is the beauty of humanity—inspiration is everywhere. As you evaluate your sources of inspiration today, take notice of how the wisdom of others can move you toward your dreams.

Remember, **hold tight to the people, places, and things that remind you of the good and that brighten your spirit when you need it most.**

DECEMBER 15

LEAN IN TO LISTENING

Dear friend,

We live in difficult times, when it feels like disconnect and divide are more palpable than ever. How can we start to bridge this gap and honor our innate human desire for connection?

As trivial as this might sound, I believe we need to start listening to one another. To be seen, heard, and understood are universal human desires. We want to feel that our presence in this world matters; we want to feel like we belong. This is true of you and every person you meet.

By really listening, we become present to someone else's lived experiences, showing that we care. And we learn a lot about people when we are present to their words, their expressions, and the energy they give. We can pick up on their pain, needs, or anxieties. How wonderful that such a seemingly simple practice can be so powerful and meaningful!

Let's refocus on this simple skill and listen with the intention of connection and understanding. When you make this effort to be present to others, you show a deeper respect for life itself. Who in your life can you give the gift of feeling seen, heard, and understood today?

Remember, **listening is a gift you give to yourself and others.**

YOU ARE ALWAYS WORTHY

Dear friend,

Did you know that your worth is innate, untouchable, and unshakable, regardless of what happens in life? I promise, this is true.

So often we allow ourselves to think our actions and mistakes detract from our worthiness. And it's natural to feel that way. Many of us were never taught to own our worth. In fact, some of us were taught the opposite: We must earn our worth. And when we have behaved confidently, in accordance with our worth, someone has always been ready to criticize us for our confidence or cut us down to size.

Today's the day to break free from living smaller than you are. It's time to rewrite how you show up in the world and flip the script on how you talk to yourself. You are worthy. Your life is important. You matter. You are here for a reason. If anyone questions that, have empathy, because it's likely they have forgotten their own worth too. You have nothing to prove or earn today.

Remember, **your worth is inherent; it cannot be taken away. You are here for a reason.**

DECEMBER 16

YOUR STORY MATTERS

Dear friend,

Years ago, I went to a public-speaking workshop about the power of storytelling, and I learned how each of us has an important story to tell. While listening to other participants, I wasn't sure my story would measure up. Before my turn, I anxiously approached the instructor, hoping to get a pass. Instead, I was guided to get out of my head and speak to my current experience: doubt, anxiety, and comparison. I pulled myself together and vulnerably shared.

I was so surprised to receive positive feedback and support from the group. Many resonated with my sentiments and felt comforted by my sharing of my experience. It was a moment of connection and unity, and all it took was a little honesty and bravery.

What's the story you're telling? Do you trust in the power and purpose of your story? As you sit with these questions, know that your voice and heart will touch people, no matter what. Your story matters.

Remember, **meaningful connection and healing come through the brave act of sharing who you are by telling your story.**

STRENGTH FROM SUFFERING

Dear friend,

As you know by now, I am a believer in letting all feelings be felt. There is great benefit in being present to our emotions and allowing them to work through us. But even with this knowledge, I find that I still frequently push away one feeling in particular: suffering.

When we're in it, or even if we're watching someone else go through it, suffering can feel nearly impossible to overcome. The weight of our suffering can make us believe we will never find our way out, so it's easy to feel drained and depleted by this pain.

Yet when we are open to it, pain and suffering can be teachers, showing us something new about ourselves and our lives. Suffering calls us in, asking us to be brave and vulnerable with our reality. Do we need to make a change? Or should we simply commit to caring for ourselves more deeply during this hard time?

Suffering can show you what actions to take when you are present to it. In difficult times, you can become a stronger version of yourself. Suffering can help light your path, showing you what really matters and where you have room to grow.

Remember, **your pain is not forever; this, too, will pass. Be gentle with yourself, now and always.**

DECEMBER 19

DEFINE YOUR PEACE

Dear friend,

We've talked a lot about peace during our time together, specifically inner peace. Today, I want to ask: What does peace look and feel like for you?

Let yourself imagine, right now, your ideal existence—one in which you feel completely at peace. Where are you? Who are you with? What are some descriptive qualities and characteristics of this idealized state? Let yourself embody this peace. How does it feel?

Now that you've visualized your peace, ask yourself, *What is one small action I can take to bring this peace into my current reality?*

Perhaps peace to you means quiet. Can you add a few minutes of quiet time into your day? Maybe you experience peace in the care of a community. How can you strengthen your relationships in your life? Knowing what peace means to you and defining it in your own unique way will allow you to be clear on how to cultivate peace and prioritize it in your day-to-day life.

Remember, **your peace is unique to you. Allow yourself the space and grace to take whatever actions are needed to cultivate more peace in your life.**

KNOW YOUR RESPONSIBILITY

Dear friend,

We all live with certain levels of privilege and status. As a child, I was taught that if you have power, it's your responsibility to share it and do good with it. While my young mind didn't totally grasp what that meant, a seed was planted within me to be compassionate and inclusive. Given the beautifully diverse nature of life, we all hold different strengths and abilities. We all can use our stature for good. Viewing the world as a global community encourages a shared responsibility to one another. It's empowering to know that our combined actions create real impact, moving us closer to a kinder, more empathetic world.

If you're faced with overwhelm or despair, remember the power of small, intentional actions. We don't have to save or change the world by ourselves, but we can do our part by sharing our gifts and lifting up those around us. Deep fulfillment comes from living from this responsibility. How you show up in this world matters.

Today, I'd like to remind you of your power to take loving actions.

Remember, **you are able to do much good in the world. Never forget your capacity and responsibility to love.**

LOOK FOR THE LIGHT

Dear friend,

Whenever you feel particularly downtrodden and your hope has dwindled, look for the light at the end of the tunnel. A flicker of hope can be your lifesaver in moments of darkness. When you remember to connect with the belief that good is on the horizon, you can start to find acceptance and hope to fuel you.

You can also remember, when things feel heavy or gloomy, that the only constant in life is change. The dynamics of today will soon be part of your past. How you're feeling right now won't last. When you remember that you are a creative being, capable of molding and shaping your life, you can bring yourself back into equilibrium again.

If you're in a chapter of struggle, what can you recall to remind yourself of the magic that's already on its way to you, as you mold and shape your life? What dream, goal, or ideal can you hold on to so you can be lifted up when you feel down? Take time to purposefully remember those dreams, and you'll find yourself feeling more hopeful, excited, and optimistic for the future.

Remember, **a light is always at the end of the tunnel. Let your hope sustain you.**

NEW IS NEVER EASY

Dear friend,

There's a lot of promise and excitement when we think of the new, whether big or small: a new job, a new car, a new pair of shoes, a new chapter of life. Imagining these possibilities fills me with optimism, even as I write this to you now.

Just as new endeavors and new chapters bring a palpable level of excitement, they can also bring feelings of fear, anxiety, and nervousness. Starting something new is never easy, and being a beginner can be hard. Release the fear of being bad when starting something new, and embrace it instead. In fact, the challenge can be the fun part, if you let it.

It's actually a good thing that new beginnings challenge us. Hardships provide opportunities to learn, grow, and evolve. Don't let the fear of a difficult fresh start keep you from making the moves you're yearning to make. Today, if you're trying a new path, let yourself be a beginner, and embrace the process of starting something new.

Remember, **it is an act of bravery to try something new. Honor your desire to begin what is sure to be a worthwhile endeavor.**

DECEMBER 23

THE MAGIC OF UNCERTAINTY

Dear friend,

Have you ever wished you had a crystal ball to catch a glimpse of your future? We all crave a sense of certainty that life will work out and everything will be okay. But the reality is, the future is never promised, and we can never be assured of what is to come. How can we learn to live within this tension, approaching our future with acceptance and optimism rather than fear?

Sure, it's natural to be afraid of the unknown. But I think part of the magic of life is not knowing it all. When we are curious, life expands. When we are afraid, it contracts. Rather than closing ourselves off from the unknown, can we seek to step into it bravely?

Today, face the unknown with confidence, knowing that you are capable of handling whatever life brings your way. You don't need to know how life will unfold; you just need to be present, from moment to moment.

Remember, **you don't have to approach the future with fear; rather, hold on to the excitement of all that can be.**

SIMPLE REFRAME, BIG SHIFT

Dear friend,

So much of what I hope to share with you in these notes is how simple reframes can create big shifts. For example, through mindfulness and presence, you can find gratitude for the life you're living now.

Sometimes we're so caught up in the results, we lose sight of what's in front of us. If you feel this anxiety start to rise, allow a practice of gratitude to bring you needed peace. Whenever you feel like life has left you behind, let gratitude be a raft to keep you afloat, knowing that no matter what, you have a reason to be grateful.

What you cherish most and find gratitude for will be your own. What delights or surprises you will be tailored to your tastes. But trust that blessings are always around you; you simply have to look for them.

You don't have to make major shifts to start experiencing the life you desire. Today, make gratitude your mindset and actively seek the tiny joys that lift you up even when things feel heavy. Notice how your mind, body, and spirit react to living with a grateful heart.

Remember, **small shifts and consistent practices breed big results. Let gratitude change your perspective.**

BE PLAYFUL

Dear friend,

As kids, we were given playtime—dedicated time in the day for curiosity, fun, and creativity. I never really realized how important this time was until I started to miss it in adulthood. Of course, with age come responsibility and stress, but there's still a place in our lives for that sense of childlike joy and playfulness.

Despite the fact that we've grown and matured, does this mean that life has to be serious and without fun? Can we partake in activities strictly for the joy it brings, with no payoff or expectation? Can we remember the important role fun and play have in our adult lives?

The antidote to a stressful and challenging life is seeking out moments of joy and allowing yourself to express lighthearted emotion. Where can you find those glimmers of playfulness and creativity in your day? Let yourself be filled with wonder and curiosity, and notice how those small shifts come out to play and impact your mood and energy.

Remember, **you don't have to close off parts of yourself just because you're an adult. Let yourself play.**

BUILD DISCIPLINE

Dear friend,

The word *discipline* doesn't exactly bring up warm, fuzzy feelings for most people. I long considered discipline to be harsh and punishing, a commitment to doing things we don't want to do. But I think we can take that word back and embrace it. Discipline doesn't have to feel like a punishment or a chore, when the routines and actions are aligned with our desires—practiced with love and care.

Over time, I've actually grown to crave discipline. I love the feeling I get from committing to something that's good for me and sticking to it. It feels good to honor and love myself in this way.

Today, ask yourself where you want to commit your time and energy. Only you can hold yourself accountable and responsible for seeing it through. Discipline is a signal of honored dreams and self-care. What does discipline look like for you?

Remember, **where you commit your time and energy is a signal of what you value.**

WHO ARE YOU BECOMING?

Dear friend,

I hope you know by now that you are a work of art—always shifting, never finished. You are changing every passing second, and your evolution is in motion whether you notice it or not.

It's kind of cool to think of our lives as an ongoing transformation, and we have the power to approach each day with optimism and curiosity for what is to come, while honoring what has passed. Every moment until now has molded and shaped you; the choices you make today will pave your path.

As you observe your personal transformation thus far, ask yourself, *Who am I becoming? What do I hope my life will be? One filled with kindness, creativity, and meaningful connections? One that emanates peace and is rooted in optimism?* Allow yourself to expand into the fullest version of you.

Set the intention for who you want to be and live inside of that. You will attract more of the energy that you put into the world, and there's something or someone out there who needs your voice and your presence. Your presence on this Earth is a gift. The world is lucky to have you.

Remember, **there's so much possibility within you, so much beauty yet to unfold.**

THE ART OF THE APOLOGY

DECEMBER 28

Dear friend,

What's your go-to when you've made a mistake? How do you make amends and repair a rift? It's not always easy to acknowledge wrongdoing, but becoming skilled at apologizing is a worthwhile endeavor.

As I've gotten older, my relationship with apologies and amends has changed. I used to view them as transactional: I did something wrong, I apologized. Case closed.

On the flip side, I often fell for fake apologies, or emotional bandages, when I had been wronged. These provided momentary fixes, but the wounds remained.

Now I view amends as a true act of love and care—a sign that you wish to make a wrong, right. Through presence and understanding, a solution can be found. When it comes to a true apology, showing that you care and committing to doing better are the true path to healing.

Remember, you are not meant to live perfectly. Own who you are, own your actions, and let the people in your life know that you care.

DECEMBER 29

RIDE THE WAVES

Dear friend,

If you look back on your life, say, over the last year, what do you see? Take stock of achievements and milestones, and let them motivate you to keep reaching for what you desire.

Perhaps you're surprised by how much you've accomplished, or maybe you're feeling disappointed. Some years are more fruitful than others. That's okay. And sometimes, you just need a little distance to appreciate how profound your accomplishments really are.

Life will always be filled with an array of experiences—sometimes the waves are choppy, and sometimes they're smooth. No matter what, you need to hone at least three qualities to get you through:

> *patience* to help you through challenging times,
> *hope* to prepare you for opportunities, and
> *acceptance* to bring you a sense of inner peace and calm.

These qualities can help you ride the waves of life, year after year, and navigate any currents that come your way. Which do you need most today? Stay in your flow and keep riding the waves.

Remember, **each part of your life, whether choppy or smooth, has purpose and meaning. Embrace each moment for the blessings it brings.**

THE STORY YOU TELL

Dear friend,

If someone were to read the story of your life, what would the takeaway be? Your life is your message, and you have control of the narrative. So today, ask yourself:

> *What is my life's theme?*
> *Who are the people in my story?*
> *How do I respond to challenges when they arrive?*
> *What's motivating to me?*
> *What impact do I make on others?*

If you are noticing themes and plotlines that don't feel aligned with who you are and what you want, know that you can start to make changes to shift your tone and message.

If your story is feeling stale, be brave and take a risk. Are you bored? Invite in something—or someone—new. Or try a new adventure and add excitement to your day. Your story is never over; you can choose to start a new chapter. What chapter will you start writing today?

Remember, in every moment of your life, you have the power to make changes and shift your story.

DECEMBER 31

EVOLVE

Dear friend,

Whenever I feel a chapter of life coming to a close, I find myself assessing where I've been, what I've done, and what else I can do. I'll ask myself, *What has changed, and what do I desire to change, moving forward?*

While processing the feelings that come up when I hear the word *change*, I realize that the word often implies something is wrong with the present version of myself. Can you relate? If so, here's a gentle reminder: That isn't true.

We can simultaneously desire to be and do better without putting down who we are in the moment. We can seek growth and expansion while simultaneously accepting where we are and trusting that our lives will evolve naturally. In fact, I like the word *evolve* better. Evolving means we can stay present to what is and maintain trust in the ever-changing nature of life.

Choosing to trust your own evolution helps to release judgment and self-criticism and replaces it with self-love and optimism. Today, affirm and reinforce your focus on your daily evolution. Celebrate the tiny, meaningful shifts that are produced through daily connection and aligned action.

Remember, **you don't have to change who you are to heal, evolve, or find peace.**

THANK YOU

Dear friend,

It's hard to believe the time has come to close out this year of growth. We've been through so much, and I'm grateful that you've spent your precious time and energy engaging in this friendship and committing to yourself.

We've learned, healed, and overcome, and though this is the last love note of this book, know that you can revisit any of these entries whenever you need to feel encouragement or support from a friend. I'll always be here for you, and I believe in who you're becoming.

Thank you for being *you*, for all that you are, and for all that you will be in this world.

ACKNOWLEDGMENTS

Writing these acknowledgments is perhaps the hardest part of this book because I feel overwhelming gratitude for so many people who have helped me on this journey to becoming a published author. I am truly grateful for every person who celebrated and cheered me on in this book-writing process.

Mom: There is no thank-you list where you are not at the top. Everything I am and everything I know are because of you. No simple thank-you will ever be enough.

Donna: I don't know where I'd be without you in my life. So much of the wisdom in this book stems from what you've instilled in me. I'm forever grateful for you.

To the people in my corner who have always seen me and believed in me, my heart is full: Iris, Louis, Yaz, Jess, Meag, Shelby, Sammy, Danielle, Nicole, Travis, Anne, Tiffany, Yasmine, Tara, Noel, Melanie, Heather, Courtney, Erika, Anne Marie, Brandin, Claudia, Anita, Molly, Christi, Casey, and Amina.

To all my teachers, mentors, and coaches: Thank you for seeing me, believing in me, and inspiring me in all ways.

To my team, who has shown me what authentic support feels like: Carrie, Rebeca, Cassandra, and Natasha.

To Jonathan: Thank you for seeing something in me and believing in my work. I'd probably still have an unpublished manuscript if not for you.

To the Harper Celebrate team: Danielle, Michael, Bonnie, and Sabryna, thank you for seeing my vision, making this labor of love so enjoyable, and being supportive.

To all my friends I've met near and far: Thank you for your connection, kindness, and care.

And last, but never least: Thank you to Charlotte, my emotional support cat, cowriter, and sidekick—the one who has been with me through it all.

NOTES

March
[1] Caroline Myss and James Finley, *Transforming Trauma: A Seven-Step Process for Spiritual Healing* (Sounds True, 2009), CD.
[2] Eckhart Tolle, *The Power of Now* (New World Library, 2004), 35–36.
[3] Sanjana Gupta, "*This* Is When Emotional Monitoring Becomes Toxic," VeryWell Mind, October 23, 2024, https://www.verywellmind.com/emotional-monitoring-8731901.

May
[1] Mary Ann Pietzker, "Is It True? Is It Necessary? Is It Kind?," in *Miscellaneous Poems* (Griffith and Farran, 1872), 54–55.

August
[1] Charles Black MD, "85% of What You Worry About Never Happens," *Medium*, August 17, 2021, https://medium.com/p/3f748aab16de.

September
[1] Nedra Glover Tawwab, *Set Boundaries, Find Peace* (Piatkus, 2021).
[2] M. Scott Peck, *The Road Less Traveled* (Simon & Schuster, 1978; repr., Rider, 2008), 3.

October
[1] Bronnie Ware, *The Top Five Regrets of the Dying: A Life Transformed by the Dearly Departing* (Hay House, 2019).

November
[1] Sarah Epstein, "What Is a Cycle-Breaker?" *Psychology Today*, July 15, 2022, https://www.psychologytoday.com/us/blog/between-the-generations/202207/what-is-a-cycle-breaker.
[2] "Gaslighting," *Psychology Today*, accessed February 20, 2025, https://www.psychologytoday.com/us/basics/gaslighting.
[3] John Mayer, "The Age of Worry," track 2 on *Born and Raised*, Columbia Records, 2012.

December
[1] Michael A. Singer, *The Surrender Experiment* (Harmony/Rodale, 2015).

ABOUT THE AUTHOR

Michelle embodies a profound passion for guiding individuals toward happiness, fulfillment, and inner peace. As the founder of the nonprofit organization Peaceful Mind Peaceful Life® and the creator of the popular podcast *Life Happens*, Michelle leads a mission to improve mental health and wellness through transformative workshops, impactful courses, and a nurturing online community.

Under her guidance, Peaceful Mind Peaceful Life® has become a leader in the space, reaching over fifty-five million people with inspirational content and practical tools that empower individuals to prioritize self-care and embrace mindfulness in their daily lives.

Together with her mother, Barb, she cohosts the podcast *Life Happens*, where they tackle life's most interesting and meaningful topics through vulnerability and shared experiences. Together, they encourage listeners to reflect on their own personal growth while discussing how to manage stress, build resilience, foster healthier relationships, and enhance overall well-being.

A sought-after keynote speaker, armed with a journalism degree from Indiana University, Michelle is not just a voice of encouragement but also a registered yoga teacher and an advocate for mindfulness, holding multiple certifications in meditation and personal empowerment.

Michelle believes that the journey to inner peace and empowerment is not about a destination—it's a powerful collective movement toward a brighter, more compassionate world.